463 HARD TO BELIEVE FACTS

By
Nayden Kostov

Contents

PROLOGUE

This book is full of fun and verified facts, presented in an accessible manner that I hope will provide you with hours of entertainment. My objective has been to provide you with a lifetime supply of icebreakers and points of discussion. Amaze your friends and family by telling them that all the planets in our Solar System could fit in the distance between Earth and the Moon or that flamingos can drink boiling water.

Following the success of my trivia website www.RaiseYourBrain.com, I published "1123 Hard to Believe Facts", which was read by tens of thousands of people and accumulated hundreds of 5-star reviews on Amazon and GoodReads. "853 Hard to Believe Facts" and "523 Hard to Believe Facts" followed and were even more successful. This instalment of the series has even more detail for each fact, as requested by previous readers (i.e., same volume, fewer facts).

These facts are a result of years of sifting through history and reference books, as well as searching the Internet and researching the news. Each fact is suitable for nearly any age – the "spiciest" entries are separated by their own chapter but still use clean language!

Become a trivia whiz with even more facts in the Hard to Believe Facts series!

CHAPTER I

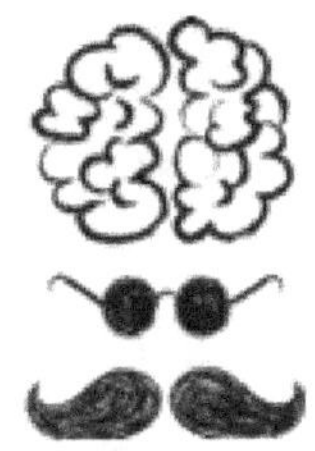

MYTH VS FACT

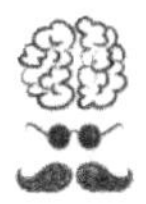

1.

Myth: When you step on a landmine, there is a soft click and it is "waiting" for you to lift your foot to explode.

Reality: When you step on a landmine, it explodes immediately.

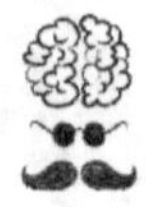

2.

Myth: Nuclear power plants release during normal operation more radiation compared to any other type of power plant.

Reality: The coal ash – a by-product from burning coal for electricity – introduces into the surrounding environment 100 times more radiation than a nuclear power plant producing the equal amount of energy. It is caused by coal's content of uranium and thorium, both radioactive elements.

3.

Myth: Parmesan cheese has a particular smell that you cannot mistake.

Reality: Blindfolded test participants often cannot distinguish between the smell of Parmesan cheese and vomit. Both have the same active chemical – butyric acid.

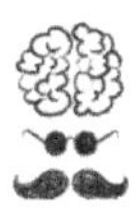

4.

Myth: We have more than enough sand.

Reality: You would not believe it, but humankind is short of sand. Sand is a crucial ingredient of concrete, which we use to construct shopping malls, offices, apartment blocks, roads, etc. Window glass at your home and silicon chips in your computer have been made of melted-down sand. One might fail to see the scarcity as a real problem as our planet is covered in it: vast deserts and coastlines around the world are lined with sand. Let me explain: we extract most of the sand to produce concrete, and for that purpose, desert sand grains are too smooth to form stable concrete. We need more angular sand, which is found in rivers, in lakes, and on the seashore. Due to the skyrocketing demand, criminal gangs all over the planet have created a black market. Additionally, sand extraction from rivers has caused billions of dollars in damage to infrastructure around the world: numerous bridges and hillside buildings have collapsed, killing hundreds of people.

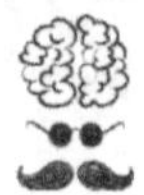

5.

Myth: The remains of a man who perished during a volcanic eruption represent a "man masturbating for one last time".

Reality: A photograph showing the remains of a man who perished during the volcanic eruption that destroyed the Roman city of Pompeii in 79 CE was repeatedly posted online with the caption "masturbating man". About 2,000 people were killed instantly when Mount Vesuvius erupted, and the city was buried in a thick carpet of volcanic ash. Due to the exorbitant heat, many of the victims experienced muscle contractions and were left frozen in a boxer-like position. These poses have nothing to do with sexual activity or masturbation.

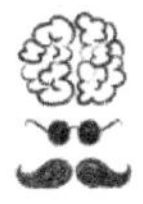

6.

Myth: Heavy cream is heavier than milk.

Reality: Do not be misled by the name: heavy cream is whipping cream with a milk fat content of between 36 and 40 percent. It is in fact lighter than milk.

7.

Myth: Michael Jackson held the rights of South Carolina's anthem.

Reality: The state of South Carolina, USA, has two official state songs: "Carolina" and "South Carolina On My Mind". The latter has a title very similar to the famous James Taylor song "Carolina In My Mind" (recorded and released on the Beatles' label, Apple Records). Michael Jackson did indeed own the rights to most of the Beatles/Apple catalogue, along with "Carolina In My Mind", but for sure not to "South Carolina On My Mind".

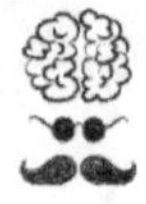

8.

Myth: The US state of West Virginia is further west than the state of Virginia.

Reality: It is exactly the opposite, check a map!

9.

Myth: The Ponzi scheme was invented by Charles Ponzi.

Reality: A Ponzi scheme is a fraud that lures investors and pays profits to earlier investors with funds from more recent investors. Among the first scams that meet the definition of a Ponzi scheme were those organised by Adele Spitzeder in Germany from 1869 to 1872, and by Sarah Howe in the USA through the so-called "Ladies' Deposit", in the 1880s. The Ponzi scheme was also previously described in novels: Charles Dickens's 1844 novel, "Martin Chuzzlewit", and his 1857 novel, "Little Dorrit", both describe such a scheme. In the 1920s, Charles Ponzi carried out this fraud and became notorious throughout the USA because of the huge amount of money that he collected.

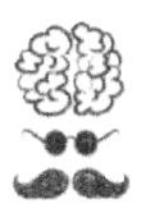

10.

Myth: The Spanish fly is a fly.

Reality: The Spanish fly was once used as an aphrodisiac. It is however not a fly, but an emerald green beetle of the species *Lytta vesicatoria*.

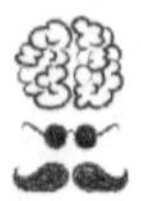

11.

Myth: Many of the Salem's witches were burned at the stake.

Reality: The Salem witch trials were a series of prosecutions of people accused of witchcraft in colonial Massachusetts, present-day USA, between February 1692 and May 1693. More than two hundred people were accused. Nineteen were hanged, several died in custody, and one was crushed to death. None of the convicted was burned at the stake.

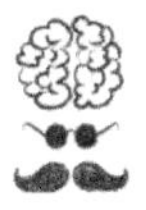

12.

Myth: The Stanford Prison Experiment of 1971, one of the most famous and compelling psychological studies of all time, told us a simple, yet scary story about human nature. The study took paid participants and assigned them to be "inmates" or "guards" in a mock prison at Stanford University, USA. Very quickly, the "guards" started mistreating the "prisoners", which implied evil is caused by circumstance. The authors concluded that innocent people, put into a situation where they enjoy power over others, will eventually abuse that power. The experiment has been mentioned in many psychology textbooks and is often cited uncritically. It has been the subject of movies, documentaries, books, television shows, and a congressional testimony.

Reality: It was revealed in 2018 that the guards in the experiment had been coached to be cruel and the experiment's most memorable moment – a prisoner heartbreakingly screaming: "I'm burning up inside!" – had been the result of pure acting.

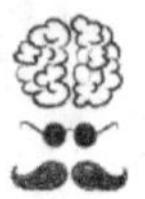

13.

Myth: The notorious drug lord, Pablo Escobar offered to repay the external debt of Colombia if the government left him alone.

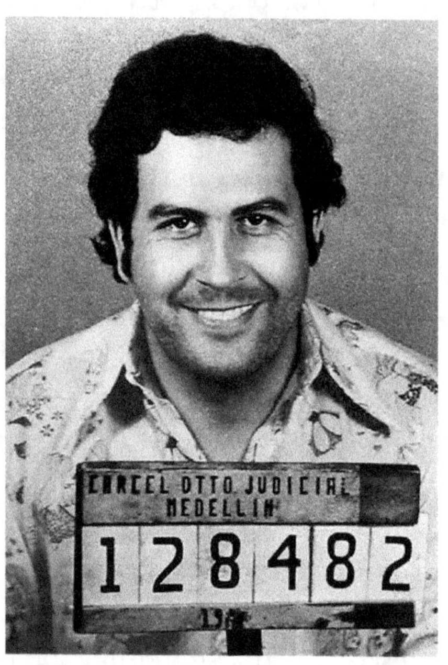

Reality: His son disproved it. The rumour started when a former President of Colombia visited Pablo Escobar and the press speculated about it.

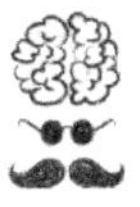

14.

Myth: The story is often told of Napoleon's army freezing in the bitter Russian Winter, their clothes falling apart as tin pest ate the buttons.

Reality: This appears to be an urban legend. Indeed, several French regiments did use tin buttons and the temperature during the Russian winter did drop low enough for a tin pest to start (below -40°C or -40°F). However, any tin that might have been used would have been quite impure, and thus more tolerant of low temperatures. According to laboratory tests, pure tin needs almost two years to develop significant tin pest damage, much longer than the duration of the entire invasion. Additionally, none of the survivors described any problem with buttons and, most probably, the legend is a mix of a real case of Russian tin buttons falling apart in an army warehouse in the 1860s and the deplorable condition of Napoleon's soldiers upon their return.

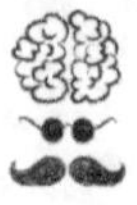

15.

Myth: Penis fish is a species of very ugly fish.

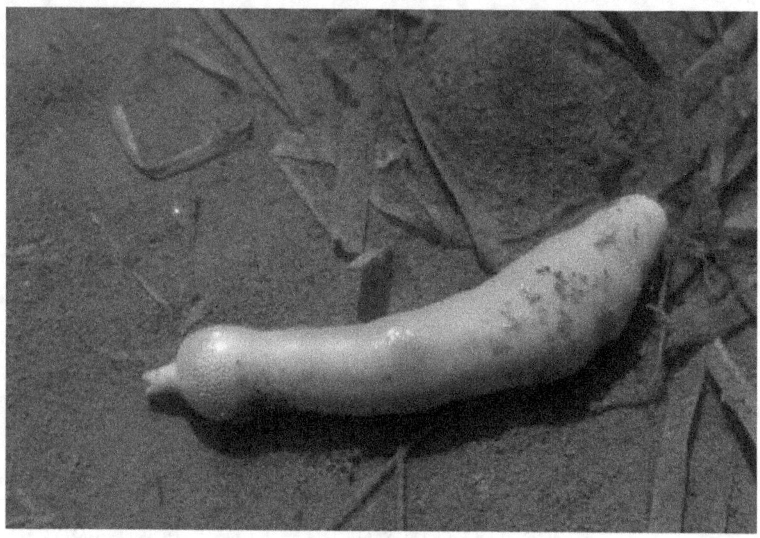

Reality: Despite its nickname, a "penis fish" is neither a penis nor a fish. It is a species of non-segmented sea worm native only to the Pacific Coast between Oregon, USA, and Baja California, Mexico.

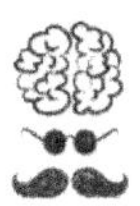

16.

Myth: Identical twins have identical DNA.

Reality: It is a common misconception: although they begin development with a matching genetic blueprint, differences in gene expression throughout life mean that they differentiate more and more as they age. Though still more similar than ordinary siblings, they are no longer identical.

17.

Myth: Black people are immune to skin cancer.

Reality: Black people and those with darker skin tones can and do get skin cancer. However, skin cancer is not a frequent occurrence among them.

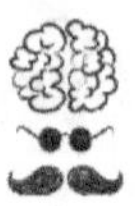

18.

Myth: The Cheops pyramid was built 1,000 years before the invention of the wheel.

Reality: The Great Pyramid of Giza (aka the Pyramid of Cheops) is the oldest and largest of the three pyramids in Giza, Greater Cairo (Egypt). It is also the oldest of the Seven Wonders of the Ancient World (built in the period 2580-2560 BCE), and the only one to remain mostly intact. The wheel had been invented some 1,000 years before that in Mesopotamia.

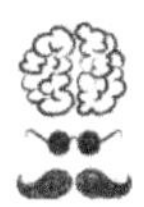

19.

Myth: In California, USA, firefighters discovered a corpse whilst assessing the damage done by a forest fire. The dead male wore a neoprene wetsuit, a dive tank, flippers and a facemask. A post-mortem confirmed that the person perished from massive internal injuries and not from burns. It was established that, on the day of the fire, the man was diving in the ocean – some 20 km (12 mi) away from the forest. The fire brigade used helicopters with very large buckets to put down the fire. The buckets were filled in the ocean where they accidentally caught the unfortunate diver and then tossed him onto the forest fire.

Reality: Fascinating as it may sound, the whole story is an over-repeated urban legend. It is simply impossible to happen as described, because of the size of the openings: Bombardier water bombers typically have two buckets protected by grilles intakes measuring 10 by 30 cm (4 by 10 in); the intake of the largest helibucket has only a 30-cm (1 ft) round opening; helitankers (choppers bearing a fixed tank) suck up water through a hose with an even smaller diameter. All those are far too narrow to get a diver through.

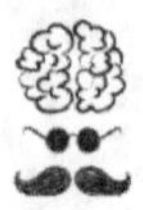

20.

Myth: Paul the Apostle was one of the Twelve Apostles.

Reality: Paul the Apostle (c. 5 CE – c. 67 CE), originally known as Saul of Tarsus, was an apostle, but not one of the Twelve Apostles.

21.

Myth: Women's mating preferences for masculinity and symmetry shift according to their menstrual cycle.

Reality: A peer-reviewed study, "Preferences across the Menstrual Cycle for Masculinity and Symmetry in Photographs of Male Faces and Bodies" found no evidence for any cyclic shift in female preferences. Correlations between attractiveness and masculinity, as well as attractiveness and symmetry did not vary materially between high and low-fertility test sessions. Furthermore, there was no measurable distinction between high and low-fertility ratings of attractiveness.

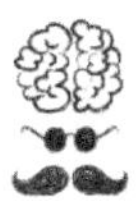

22.

Myth: You write on the blackboard with chalk.

Reality: Blackboard and sidewalk chalk were originally made from the sedimentary rock of the same name, a form of soft limestone. Today, sidewalk and blackboard chalk are made from gypsum as it is more common and easier to work with than chalk.

23.

Myth: You can multitask.

Reality: There is no such thing as multitasking. As numerous studies have confirmed, the true multitasking – i.e., performing more than one task at the same time – is a myth. Those people who think they can split their attention between multiple tasks at once are not actually getting more done. In reality, they become more stressed out, and have a lower overall productivity than those who single-task.

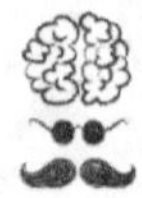

24.

Myth: Tulips originated in Holland.

Reality: Originally cultivated in the Ottoman Empire (present-day Turkey), tulips were imported into Holland in the 16th century.

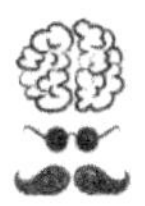

25.

Myth: A blue light is used on a crime scene to search for invisible blood.

Reality: Blood does not fluoresce by applying UV or visible blue light. Blood – even in minute quantities that remain after clean-up – can be made to "luminesce" or simply "glow in the dark" by spraying certain chemicals such as Luminol, but adding blue light is not necessary. UV alternate light sources can however detect the following: seminal fluid, saliva, and urine stains.

26.

Myth: Carrot is a fruit in the European Union (EU).

Reality: The whole "carrot as fruit" argument seems to be based on an EU trade regulation that considers carrots as fruit for tax purposes. In fact, the regulation considers carrot jam in the same category as fruit jams. That is quite different from proclaiming the carrot a fruit.

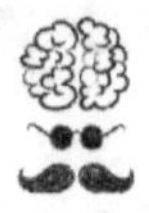

27.

Myth: Passing gas is unpleasant, but harmless.

Reality: A fart can burn you badly. In 2016, an unnamed woman was undergoing surgery at Tokyo Medical University Hospital, Japan, which involved a laser being applied to her cervix. She passed gas, which was ignited by the laser, setting, in turn, the surgical drape on fire and causing severe burns to the patient.

28.

Myth: Florence Nightingale, the pioneer of modern nursing, invented the pie chart.

Reality: In fact, she just popularised it during the Crimean War (1853-56). The earliest known pie chart was created by Scottish engineer and political economist, William Playfair, in 1801.

CHAPTER II

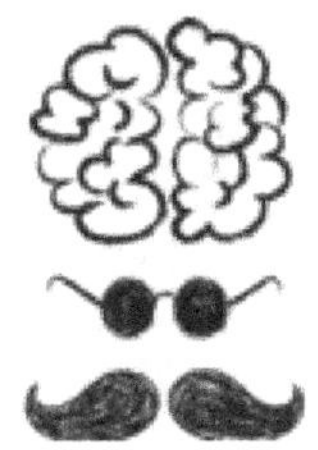

FACTS ABOUT HUMAN AND ANIMAL SEXUALITY

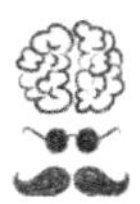

29.

The male red-capped manakin do the "moonwalk" to impress the ladies. This bird's dancing skills are one of the most impressive in the animal kingdom. Find a video online, it is worth watching.

30.

The emperor penguin is the only penguin species that breeds during the harsh Antarctic winter. It is also unique because the male is responsible for hatching the egg. Penguins walk up to 120 km (75 mi) over the ice to reach the breeding colonies, which can contain thousands

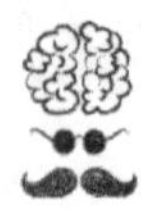

of couples. The female goes back to the sea to feed after laying one egg, which is then hatched by the male. The male spends the pitch-black, turbulent winter incubating the egg in his brood pouch. By the time the egg hatches (some 2.5 months later), the male will have fasted for around 120 days since arriving at the colony. To survive the fierce winds of up to 200 km/h (120 mph), the males huddle together, taking turns in the middle of the group. In the four months of travel, courtship, and incubation, the male may lose as much as 20 kg (44 lb) from the initial mass of 38 kg (84 lb).

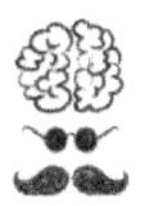

31.

The male White-fronted Parrot (also known as "White-fronted Amazon" or "Spectacled Amazon Parrot") will vomit in the female's mouth during their mating ritual. After selecting a satisfactory partner, the two parrots will start "kissing" one another, locking their beaks and playing with each other's tongues, making these birds one of the few animals to engage in kissing. During the kissing session, the male will vomit into the female's mouth.

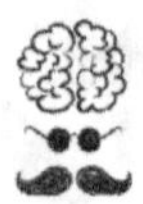

32.

"Cinq à sept" (literally "five to seven", also written "5 à 7"or "5@7") is a French term for activities happening after work and before returning home. In Quebec French (Canada), the term stands for a social gathering. The English equivalent might be an informal "happy hour". In France, however, it is a metonym for visiting one's mistress, an extramarital affair, and the mistress involved. It derives from the time of day French people would make such a visit.

33.

Female giraffes are known to urinate in the male's mouth before mating so that the male can decide if the female is a suitable mating partner.

34.

A scientist in Antarctica managed to find a date through Tinder (a geosocial networking and online dating application) with another scientist who was camping 45 minutes away.

35.

As US strippers could not work during the 2020 coronavirus lockdown, some started delivering food topless.

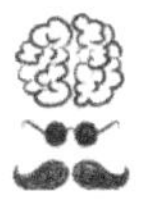

36.

An erect elephant penis can weigh as much as 30 kg (65 lb).

37.

In 2019, the Supreme Court of India ruled that sex on a false promise of marriage constitutes rape.

38.

Male echidnas have a four-headed penis. During mating, the heads on one side "shut down" and do not grow; the other two are used to release semen into the female's two-branched reproductive tract. Each time males copulate, they alternate heads in sets of two.

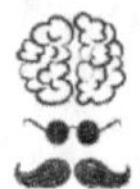

39.

Some species of fruit flies can produce coiled-up sperm more than 5 cm (2 in) long, which is 20 times the length of their own body. That is a thousand times longer in relative terms than human sperm.

40.

The directors of "The Matrix" are Larry and Andy Wachowski, who used to be brothers. Today, Lana Wachowski (born 1965 and formerly known as Larry) and Lilly Wachowski (born 1967 and formerly known as Andy) are both trans women and, technically, sisters.

41.

In 2015, China banned showing LGBT relationships on TV.

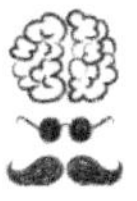

42.

According to the Canadian Journal of Psychiatry, one in twenty people taking the anti-depressant clomipramine have an orgasm when they yawn.

43.

Once female blue crabs reach sexual maturity, they mate with a male only once. Male crabs will mate with multiple females during their lifespan.

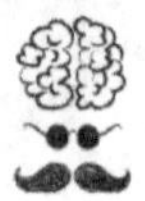

44.

In 2008, US police arrested a 40-year-old man for having sex with a picnic table. Art Price Jr. of Bellevue, Ohio, was videotaped on four separate occasions by a neighbour while "engaging sexually with a metal table".

45.

In the period 2016-18, a 47-year-old French man engaged in some 220 masturbation sessions while driving his car on the highway. Eventually, he was fined €500 ($550).

46.

In 2019, porn actress, Amaranta Hank, opened the world's first University of Porn in Colombia.

47.

Since 2019, it is OK for women to bathe topless in city-run pools in Barcelona, Spain.

48.

A "lavender marriage" is a male-female union that is in fact a marriage of convenience, aiming to conceal the sexual orientation of one or both partners.

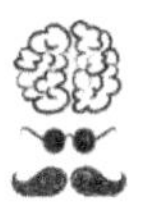

49.

In 2018, Sergio Lazarovich, a 59-year-old Argentine tax official, legally changed the last letter of his name to Sergia, assuming the identity of a woman. He did this so he could retire five years early. Local laws allow women to retire at 60, while men have to work until the age of 65. In Argentina, people can legally change their gender without any sex reassignment surgery.

50.

Balkan sworn virgins (in Albanian: Burrnesha) are women who wear male clothing and swear to abstain from sexual relationships in order to spend their life as men in northern Albania, Kosovo, Montenegro, and in other parts of the western Balkans. It is estimated that there are fewer than 100 sworn virgins left. Burrnesha is believed to be the only formal, socially defined trans masculine role in Europe.

51.

According to a 2011 study conducted in Israel, women's tears contain a chemical signal that lowers testosterone levels and dampens both sexual desire and aggression in men. They examined the effect on men of smelling fresh tears, which the researchers collected from women watching weepy movies.

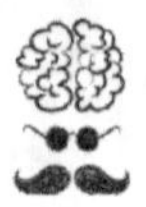

52.

Girls in Salinas, the Dominican Republic, turn male and grow penises when they enter puberty due to a rare genetic disorder. Approximately 1% of the children born in this village experience this transition by the time they reach 12. It is so common that it is no longer perceived as abnormal and the youngsters are simply called "guevedoces" – which literally means "penis at 12".

53.

In 2019, a Russian man sued Apple for making him gay. He asserted that a crypto-currency called "GayCoin" was delivered via a smartphone app, rather than the Bitcoin he had ordered. According to his testimony, the GayCoin crypto-currency came along with a message saying: "Don't judge until you try". "I thought, in truth, how can I judge something without trying? I decided to try same-sex relationships," the plaintiff explained. "Now I have a boyfriend and I do not know how to explain this to my parents."

54.

To combat malaria, Singapore released millions of "castrated" mosquitoes that mate with normal ones but do not reproduce.

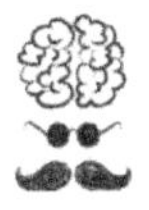

55.

The longest-lived vertebrate is the Greenland shark. These sharks live over 400 years, and reach sexual maturity at the age of about 150.

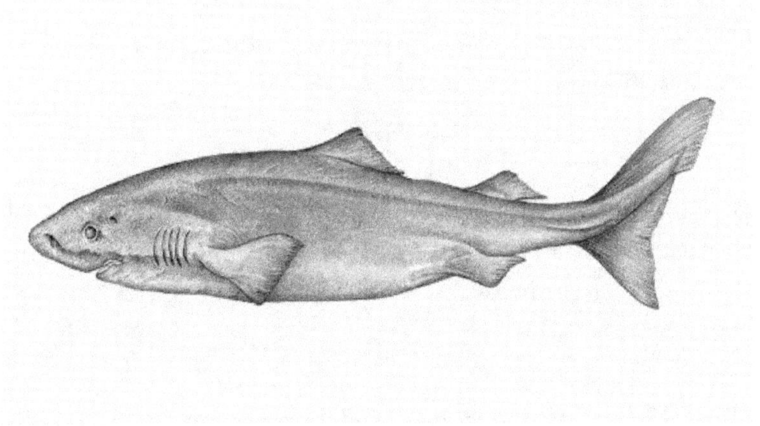

56.

In early 2020, Indonesian student, Reynhard Sinaga, the most prolific rapist in the history of the United Kingdom, was imprisoned for life for sexually assaulting 48 men. In the period 2015-17, he approached drunk men in bars and invited them to his flat, where he filmed many of the forced sexual encounters.

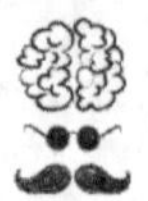

57.

Pornhub, the most famous porn website, gave Italians free Premium Access during COVID-19 quarantine in early 2020.

58.

In many US states the controversial gay conversion therapy is still legal.

59.

A deaf man sued the porn website Pornhub for lack of subtitles, claiming that, due to disabilities, he was missing the plot in the movies.

60.

Until 1979, Sweden considered homosexuality as an illness. People protested by calling in sick for feeling gay.

61.

Suicide rates dropped after gay marriage was legalised in Sweden and Denmark.

62.

In the majority of the Western countries, it is a widespread perception that homosexuals wear an earring on the right ear.

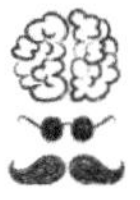

63.

If you are elected to the US Congress, you get a free copy of the porn magazine, Hustler – whether you want it or not. Following complaints from 264 congressional offices in 1984, the US Postal Service asked the US District Court for the District of Columbia to block the mailings. The court ruled, however, that the delivery of the magazine could not be stopped.

64.

A man who donated sperm to a lesbian couple is the legal father of their daughter and must pay child support, a judge in the US state of Kansas ruled in 2014. The same-sex couple had found Mr William Marotta on the Internet and did not use a doctor in the donation process. They explicitly signed a contract agreeing that Mr Marotta would bear no financial responsibility for the child. However, when the couple applied for benefits, the state requested a court to declare Mr Marotta the child's father and thus to make him financially responsible. In Kansas, a man is considered a sperm donor only if he goes through the process using the services of a doctor.

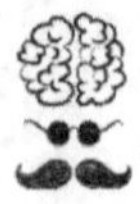

65.

In May 2020, the Dutch National Institute for Public Health and the Environment advised single men and women in the Netherlands to find a "seksbuddy" (sex buddy) for the duration of the COVID-19 lockdown.

CHAPTER III

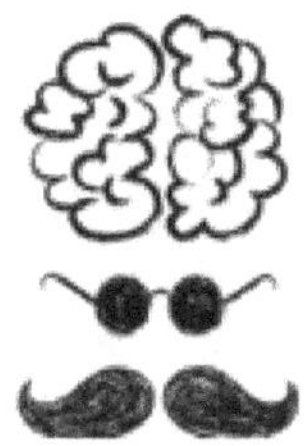

UNBELIEVABLE FACTS ABOUT VIRTUALLY EVERYTHING

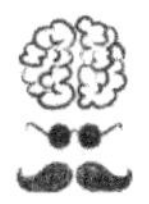

66.

Flying from west to east is usually faster than flying the same route east to west. This is due to the jet stream, a high-altitude type of wind, predominantly blowing from the west to the east. That is why airplanes flying at a constant airspeed go faster when travelling eastwards. In 2016, this inspired Air India to change the direction of its Delhi-San Francisco flight. Instead of flying west, it started flying east, adding 1,400 km (870 mi) in distance but saving two hours of flight time.

67.

If you have friends, you live a longer and healthier life than people who are alone.

68.

Beauty sleep is a real thing. According to researchers, people who miss out on sleep appear less attractive to others. A couple of bad nights is enough to make a person look "significantly" uglier, sleep experiments suggest.

69.

Over 200,000 belated Valentine's Day text messages (SMS) arrived on 7 November 2019 in the USA.

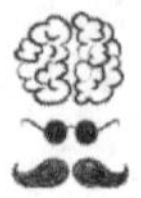

70.

As a weird experiment, in 2009, Professor Stephen Hawking organised a lavish party with lots of expensive champagne and hors d'oeuvres open to everyone, but did not announce it until the day after the party had taken place. As expected, no one attended the party. Professor Hawking was trying to prove and did so successfully that time travel is not possible.

71.

Joseph John Thomson discovered the electron. Thomson's student Ernest Rutherford discovered the proton. Rutherford's student James Chadwick discovered the neutron.

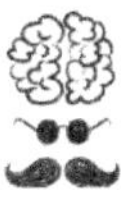

72.

A turbojet train is a train powered by jet airplane engines. Several were built for experimental purposes in the USA and the USSR. In 1966, the USA created the fastest one, reaching 296 km/h (184 mph).

73.

After decades of continuous use, the US Air Force finally retired its floppy disk system for managing nuclear weapons in 2019. The Strategic Automated Command and Control system no longer runs on 8-inch floppy drives from circa 1972.

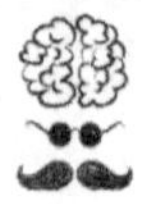

74.

In 1887, Susanna Salter became the first female mayor in the USA. Men from her town had put her on the ballot as a sexist joke, not expecting her to win.

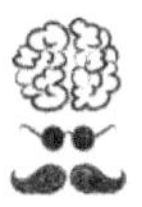

75.

What happens when you mix green and red? The overwhelming majority of women but only about half of the men know that the resulting colour is brown.

76.

Believe it or not, 2520 is the smallest number that can be divided by 1 to 10 without a fractional leftover.

77.

The Creation of Adam (Italian: Creazione di Adamo) is a part of the Sistine Chapel's ceiling. Italian artist Michelangelo painted it in the 1510s. If you look carefully, you will see that the artist hid in it a picture of the human brain.

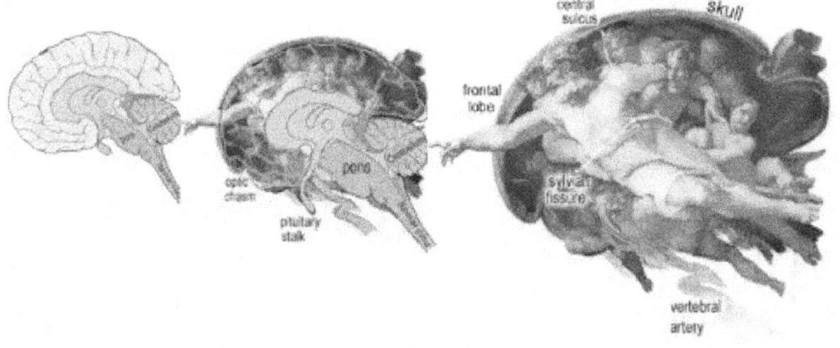

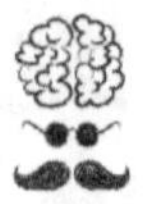

78.

The term "Asian flush" describes people's face and neck turning red when they drink alcohol. Sometimes, the red colour comes along with headache and nausea. The culprit is the deficiency of an enzyme called aldehyde dehydrogenase 2 (ALDH2). Almost half of East Asians (Chinese, Japanese, and Koreans) have this condition.

79.

Long before becoming the closely guarded tourist attraction that it is today, the Hollywood Sign (formerly known as the Hollywoodland Sign) was a slowly deteriorating advertisement for a real estate development that no one had ever cared to take down. The founder of Playboy magazine, Hugh Hefner, saved it twice. By the way, Google deliberately leads you to the wrong place if you enter "Hollywood Sign" for navigation.

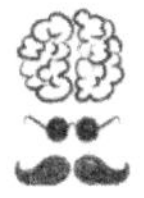

80.

You clap your dominant hand towards the other hand.

81.

Up until the 1950s, some cars had trafficators instead of blinkers. Trafficators are semaphore-like signals that stick out from the door pillars to show an intention to turn.

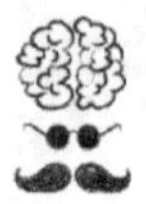

82.

In February 2020, a massive storm battering the UK helped a British Airways airplane from New York to London beat the record for the fastest subsonic transatlantic flight. Instead of the normal 6 hours and 30 minutes, it took only 4 hours and 56 minutes.

83.

US insurance company SquareMouth gave $10,000 to a client who had checked the fine print in the contract. Ms Donelan Andrews read her contract thoroughly and was the first to claim the prize by email. "Pays to Read", read the contract. SquareMouth estimated that less than 1 percent of people who buy a travel insurance policy actually read their contract and the company included the hidden prize in a bid to change that.

84.

In October 1994, Forrest Gump, Jurassic Park, Pulp Fiction, and The Shawshank Redemption were all in the movie theatres at the same time.

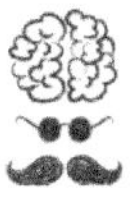

85.

In February 2020, a 62-year-old former US Marine named George Hood broke the world planking record with a time of 8 hours, 15 minutes and 15 seconds. He had done approximately 2,100 hours of planking in preparation.

86.

In early 2020, scientists published a paper claiming they had found extra-terrestrial protein in a meteorite. Using state-of-the-art mass spectrometry, they detected what they believe to be protein in the meteorite called Acfer 086, found in Algeria back in 1990.

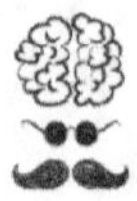

87.

The Bialbero di Casorzo (from Italian: "double tree of Casorzo"), aka Grana Double Tree, is situated between Grana and Casorzo in Piedmont, Italy. It is a mulberry tree with a cherry tree growing out of it.

88.

In November 2019, Britons Steve and Lenka Thomson won a £105 million EuroMillions jackpot ($140 million, €115 million). Steve, a builder by occupation, continued working without charging clients, urging them to buy themselves Christmas presents with the saved money.

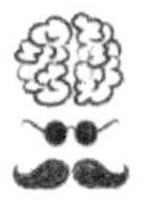

89.

In Tibetan Buddhism there are 108 sins or 108 delusions of the mind. They include, among others (caution, rare words ahead!): callousness, capriciousness, censoriousness, conceitedness, contempt, debasement, dipsomania, effrontery, furtiveness, haughtiness, imperiousness, insatiability, insidiousness, intransigence, lecherousness, ostentatiousness, prodigality, quarrelsomeness, rapacity, voluptuousness, etc.

90.

In early 2020, a German man tricked Google Maps by using a handcart full of smartphones to fool the app's algorithm into creating a virtual traffic jam. Simon Weckert searched for directions within the app on 99 second-hand smartphones, and then walked them all in a handcart through several main crossroads in Berlin, Germany.

91.

If you slowly put sugar into water, counterintuitively, the water level does not rise and remains unchanged. Dissolved into water, sugar molecules go into the spaces between the water molecules.

92.

Over 90% of us first put the left sock on.

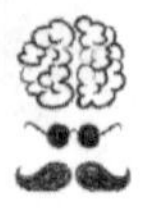

93.

Mayonnaise originated in the 14th century in what is to-day Spain.

94.

The so-called Center of the Universe in Tulsa, Oklahoma (USA), is an acoustic phenomenon. If you stand on it and make a noise, the sound is echoed back much louder than it was made.

95.

In 1843, Scottish Alexander Bain invented the first fax machine.

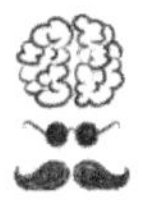

96.

The increased demand for boarding schools in the UK was called "the Harry Potter effect".

97.

There is a superstition in Hollywood that putting a question mark in the title of the film will make it a failure at the box office.

98.

The US internet sales company, Amazon, was initially named Cadabra and sold books only. The owner, Jeff Bezos, later changed the name to Amazon.com after a lawyer misheard its original name as "cadaver". The first book sold on the website was "Fluid Concepts and Creative Analogies: Computer Models of the Fundamental Mechanisms of Thought" by Douglas Hofstadter.

99.

Bitcoin was invented in 2008 by an unknown person using the alias Satoshi Nakamoto. By the way, the smallest Bitcoin unit is called a "satoshi". The first Bitcoin block was mined in early 2009.

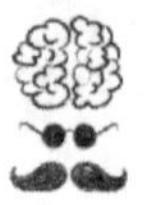

100.

Shuttle Enterprise received its name after pressures by Star Trek fans. It was initially planned to be named Constitution.

101

Joshua Abraham Norton (1818-1880), aka Emperor Norton, was a citizen of San Francisco, California (USA), who proclaimed himself "Norton I, Emperor of the United States" and "Protector of Mexico". Norton had no formal political power, but currency issued in his name was honoured in the establishments that he frequented. While considered eccentric, to say the least, the vast majority of people in San Francisco enjoyed his imperial stature. His fellow citizens were particularly amused by Norton's proclamations, some of which "dissolved" the US Congress, others urged for the construction of a bridge and tunnel to connect San Francisco with Oakland across San Francisco Bay.

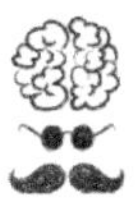

102.

Watkin's Tower (aka Watkin's Folly, the Wembley Park Tower, the Wembley Tower, the Metropolitan Tower, and the London Stump) was a metal tower in London, England, which remained unfinished. It was an ambitious attempt to create a 358-metre-high (1,175 ft) attraction in Wembley Park, advocated by the railway entrepreneur, Sir Edward Watkin. "The Great Tower of London" was meant to surpass the height of the Eiffel Tower in Paris. The project was never finalised and the half-built tower was eventually pulled down in 1907, making space for the English national football ground, Wembley Stadium.

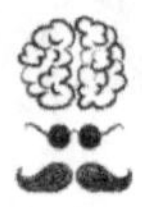

103.

Otto Frederick Rohwedder of Davenport, Iowa (USA), invented the first single loaf bread-slicing machine in 1928. By the way, early sliced bread advertisements contained instructions on how to use the bread.

104.

Susan Alice Bennett (born in 1949) is a US voice-over artist. Maybe you have never heard her name, but definitely have heard her voice – she is the female American voice of Apple's virtual assistant "Siri" since the service was introduced on iPhone 4S in 2011.

105.

Mess frees us to think more creatively and without constraint. Psychologist Kathleen Vohs from the University of Minnesota, USA, did the following experiment, in which test subjects were placed in one of two rooms. The first room was clean, clutter-free and organized. The second was messy and cluttered. The test subjects were asked to provide alternative uses for ping pong balls. People in the clean room demonstrated more conventional thinking when it came to creative uses for ping pong balls. Conversely, the test subjects in the messy room came up with crazier and more creative ping pong ball ideas.

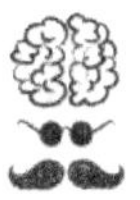

106.

Gerald Holtom designed the modern peace sign for the British Campaign for Nuclear Disarmament in 1958. The downward lines on either side of the vertical line represent the flag semaphore signal for the letter N (for nuclear) and the vertical line itself represents the semaphore signal for the letter D (disarmament).

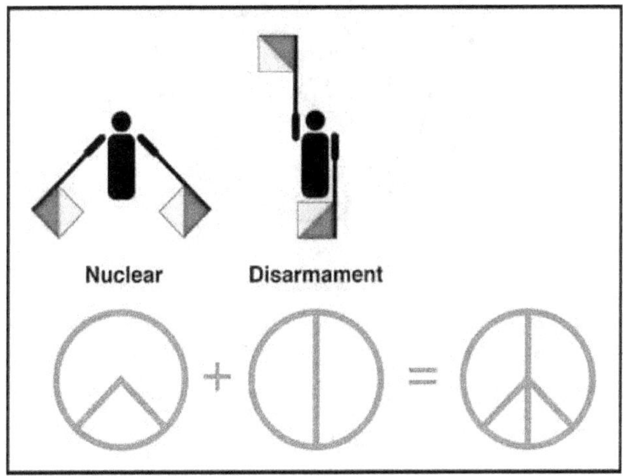

107.

Nicotine was named after a person — Jean Nicot (1530-1604). He was a French diplomat and scholar, famous for being the first to bring tobacco to France, including snuff tobacco.

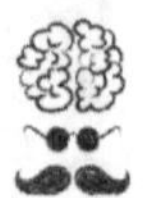

108.

The power ON/OFF button you see on every electric appliance has a 0 and a 1 hidden inside the symbol.

109.

If you pass an electric current through a pickled cucumber, it will start glowing. Many spectacular videos illustrating this phenomenon are available online.

110.

In a bid to reduce plastic waste, many bars worldwide started using pasta straws.

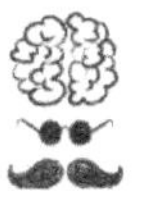

111.

"Ribs" (Russian: "ryobra"), aka "music on ribs" or "jazz on bones", are home-made gramophone records manufactured from X-ray negatives. Popular in the 1950s and 1960s, ribs were a clandestine method of smuggling in and distributing prohibited music by foreign musicians banned from broadcast in the Soviet Union, such as Elvis Presley, the Beatles, the Rolling Stones, the Beach Boys, Ella Fitzgerald, and Chubby Checker. Real medical X-rays, purchased or picked out of the trash from hospitals and clinics were used to create the recordings, whose quality was awful, but the price was low. The discs could only be played five to ten times.

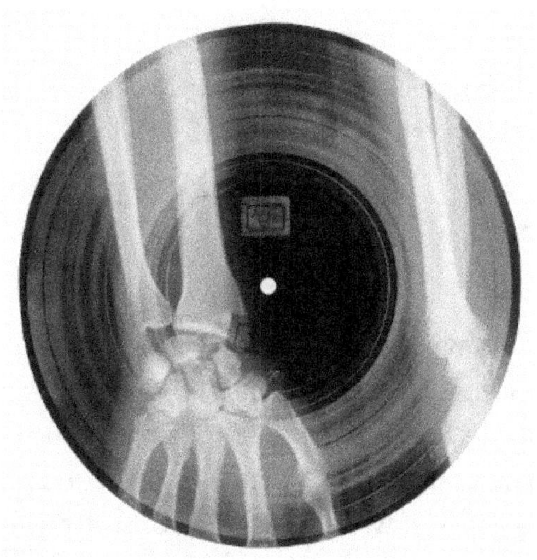

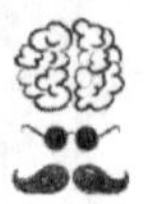

112.

At a traffic stop, US police officers are trained to never pass between the stopped vehicle and the patrol car.

113.

Dave MacPherson became Disneyland's first visitor ever in July 1955. In honour of the event, he was later rewarded with a lifetime pass.

114.

Sounds weird, but there are more planets inhabited by robots than planets inhabited by humans.

115.

Ethan Zuckerman (born 1973) is a US media scholar, blogger, and Internet activist. In 1994, he invented pop-up ads. Some 20 years later, he apologised for his creation.

116.

Johann Jacob Schweppe (1740-1821) was a German-Swiss scientist who first manufactured bottled carbonated mineral water. He produced his own carbon dioxide, whose addition was considered, at the time, to have medicinal properties. You know for sure the brand he established: Schweppes.

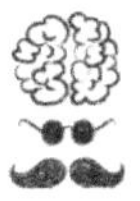

117.

Felix Baumgartner (born in 1969) is an Austrian skydiver and BASE jumper. He jumped from a helium balloon from the stratosphere on 14 October 2012 and landed in New Mexico, USA. He managed to set world records for sky-diving from an estimated 39 km (24 mi) and for reaching a top speed of 1,357.6 km/h (843.6 mph), or Mach 1.25. He is the first person to have broken the sound barrier in free-fall parachute jump.

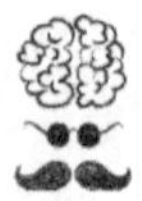

118.

Michelangelo di Lodovico Buonarroti Simoni (1475-1564), better known as simply Michelangelo, was a Renaissance painter, sculptor, and architect in the Republic of Florence. Michelangelo created his signature statue David from a block of marble that had been twice refused by other sculptors (Agostino di Duccio and Antonio Rossellino). When Michelangelo finally got his hands on it, the marble had been lying around for 40 years.

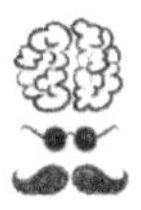

119.

Elizabeth Blackwell (1821-1910) was a British physician. She remained in the history as the first woman to receive a medical degree in the USA, and the first woman on the Medical Register of the UK's General Medical Council. Blackwell played a decisive role in both the United States and the United Kingdom to promote education for women in medicine.

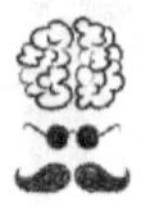

120.

The Reformation (aka the Protestant Reformation or the European Reformation) was a movement in 16th-century Europe, which challenged the authority of the Roman Catholic Church. During this period, many monasteries were closed. As an unexpected side effect, honey supply in Europe plummeted, as monks were the largest beekeepers.

121.

Concrete was known to the ancient world as early as 700 BCE. Ancient Romans used concrete extensively from 300 BCE to 476 CE. After the fall of the Roman Empire however, humankind quickly "forgot" this technology. British engineer John Smeaton "reinvented" concrete in the 1750s.

122.

Ruby is red and sapphire is blue. Yet, both gemstones are varieties of the same mineral – corundum.

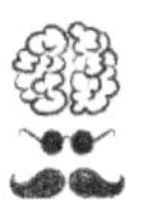

123.

Stanislav Stanislavovich Shushkevich (born in 1934) is a Belarusian politician and scientist. He served as the first head of state of independent Belarus after it seceded from the Soviet Union (1991-94). A little-known fact is that in the early 1960s, while working as an engineer in an electronics factory in Minsk, Shushkevich was giving Russian lessons to Lee Harvey Oswald. The infamous assassin of US President J.F. Kennedy fled to the Soviet Union in late 1959 and lived in Minsk until mid-1962, when he returned to the USA and eventually settled in Dallas, Texas.

124.

Xenophon Zolotas (1904-2004) was an interim non-party Prime Minister of Greece. Some of his speeches in English at the International Bank for Reconstruction and Development are considered to be historic and notable because they contained mainly terms of Greek origin. You can find the text of his speeches online and, I promise, you will not regret.

125.

Dromomania was a historical psychiatric diagnosis characterized with an uncontrollable desire to wander. The term is also used to describe an urge for frequent travelling or wanderlust.

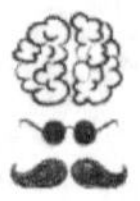

126.

Karl Heinrich Marx (1818-1883) was a German philosopher, economist, political theorist, and socialist revolutionary. His best-known works are the "The Communist Manifesto" and "Das Kapital". He died stateless and poverty-stricken with fewer than a dozen mourners attending his funeral. His last words reportedly were: "Go away! Last words are for fools who haven't said enough!"

127.

In the course of the last decades, whenever an economic crisis started in Asia, Singapore was always the first to enter into recession.

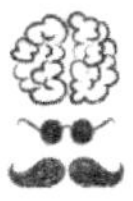

128.

A wigwam and a tipi, also spelled teepee, are two different dwellings used by Native Americans. The vast majority of people living outside the USA cannot distinguish them.

129.

US astronauts have been allowed to vote from space since 1997.

130.

US Conservatives prefer purebred dogs, poetry that rhymes, and typical food, while Liberals go for ethnic food, mixed-breed pets, and are okay with free verse.

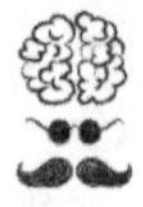

131.

In 1987, an investment banker named Steve Rothstein paid $233,510 for an American Airlines "unlimited AAir-pass". The program (now re-branded as AirPass) initially enabled pass-holders unlimited first-class travels on any of the airline's flights worldwide. A few years later, he paid further $150,000 to add a companion ticket, so he would always be able to bring a friend. Until late 2008, when his pass was cancelled, he had travelled more than 14,000,000 miles during over 10,000 flights. He cost the airline more than $21 million.

132.

In 2018, researchers at the University of British Columbia, Canada, found a technique that could make all donated blood compatible with all patients, regardless of the blood type of the donor or the recipient. They managed to convert blood types A, B, and AB into the universal type 0.

133.

People tend to prefer people born on the same date. An abnormally high number of married couples share the same birthdate.

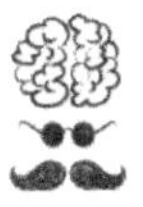

134.

Bass Reeves (1838-1910) was the first black deputy US marshal west of the Mississippi River. During his long career, he arrested over 3,000 felons and killed 14 people in self-defence. He achieved all this without being wounded a single time. Born in slavery, he remained illiterate all his life, but possessed great memory and memorised the warrants before each mission. At one instance, he arrested his own son for murder. Reeves ostensibly served as inspiration for the character of the Lone Ranger.

135.

Soviet cosmonauts carried guns in outer space. Weapons were to be used upon landing, if attacked by bears.

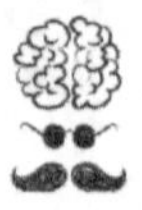

136.

Pneumatic tubes are transportation systems, which move cylindrical containers by compressed air or partial vacuum. They became popular in the late 19th and early 20th centuries and transported mail, documents, or money within a building or between adjacent buildings. Still today, they find wide use in numerous hospitals. Historically, several pneumatic transportation systems were capable of sending more sizeable cargo and even aspired to supersede the freight trains, but never gained wide acceptance. As of this writing, intensive research into passenger trains moving in partial vacuum, such as the Vactrain and Hyperloop, is ongoing.

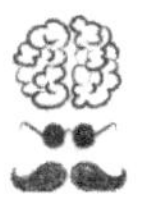

137.

Tu Youyou is a Chinese chemist who received a Nobel Prize in 2015. She developed several efficient medicines for malaria, saving millions of lives worldwide. If you think about it, she is maybe the most confusing person to sing the song "Happy Birthday to You" to.

138.

The least attractive colour is called PANTONE 448C. It is described as a "drab dark brown" and is often used on plain packaging for cigarettes.

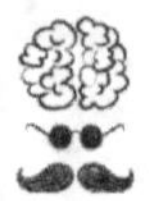

139.

The Vegetable Orchestra (in German: "Das erste Wiener Gemüseorchester") is an Austrian musical group who plays instruments produced entirely from fresh vegetables. The group, founded in 1998 in Vienna, consists of ten musicians, one sound technician, and one cook.

140.

People place more value on objects they built themselves. It is called the IKEA effect.

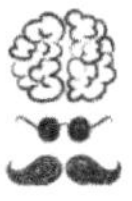

141.

Lego produced more than 300 million tires in 2011. This makes them the world's largest tire manufacturer by number of tires.

142.

Islamic banking is not allowed to invest in alcohol, arms trading, pornography, or gambling. Sharia-compliant financial products exist in many countries. Debts on Islamic credit cards, for instance, are not accumulating interest, but rather are paid by a fixed service charge.

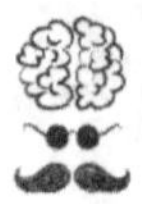

143.

Thomas Andrew "Colonel Tom" Parker (1909-1997) was Elvis Presley's manager. Their symbiosis was quite successful, Elvis being a new face in popular music, and Parker – an entrepreneur able to market him. Parker signed a merchandising deal that brought them hundreds of millions of dollars and even came up with the idea to market "I Hate Elvis" badges to make money from those who otherwise would not have parted with their cash.

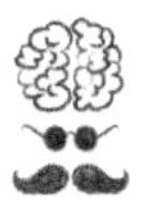

144.

A sculpture representing the head of Darth Vader is located at the Washington National Cathedral in Northwest, Washington, DC (USA). It is on the north, or "dark", side of the cathedral.

145.

Nobody knows for sure the origin of the word "posh". The best known and most widely believed story is that it comes from old-time ship travel from Great Britain to India on the packet boats run by the Peninsular and Oriental Steamship Company. It supposedly stood for "Port Out, Starboard Home".

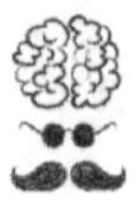

146.

The original Ferris wheel was built by George Washington Gale Ferris Jr. as the symbol of the 1893 World's Exposition in Chicago, USA. Ferris wheels quickly became the most common type of amusement ride at state fairs in the United States, and in many countries worldwide.

147.

The largest Ferris wheel in an enclosed architectural design was presented in 2012 in Ashgabat, Turkmenistan. It measured 47.6 m (156 ft) in height.

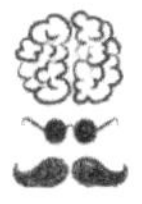

148.

The Throne of Weapons is an unconventional sculpture created by Cristóvão Canhavato out of obsolete weapons. It is owned by the British Museum and has been dubbed the Museum's most "eloquent object".

149.

In 2014, "Track 3" from Taylor Swift's album "1989" shot to No. 1 on iTunes in Canada after being released. The release was an accident, and the track is simply eight seconds of white noise. The track was subsequently removed.

150.

Investors check the stock market more frequently when it goes up.

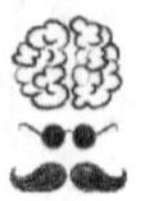

151.

The Speyer wine bottle is a sealed vessel, presumed to contain liquid wine, and so named because it was unearthed near Speyer, Germany, from a 4th-century CE Roman nobleman's tomb. It is known as the oldest bottle of wine worldwide.

152.

"Hayabusa" (*"peregrine falcon"* in Japanese) was a space probe developed by the Japan Aerospace Exploration Agency. It was the first ever to return a sample of material from an asteroid to Earth. Hayabusa was launched in 2003, and two years later, it landed on a small near-Earth asteroid named 25143 Itokawa. It collected samples, which were returned to Earth aboard the spacecraft in 2010.

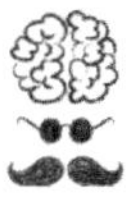

153.

In 2005, Ivan Ivanov designed the so-called Bulgarian Bag, a piece of equipment beneficial for both upper and lower body training. The leather sand-filled bags weigh anywhere from 5 kg (11 pounds) to 23 kg (50 pounds). Ivanov was inspired by the ancient tradition of Bulgarian shepherds to carry weak sheep and lambs around their shoulders.

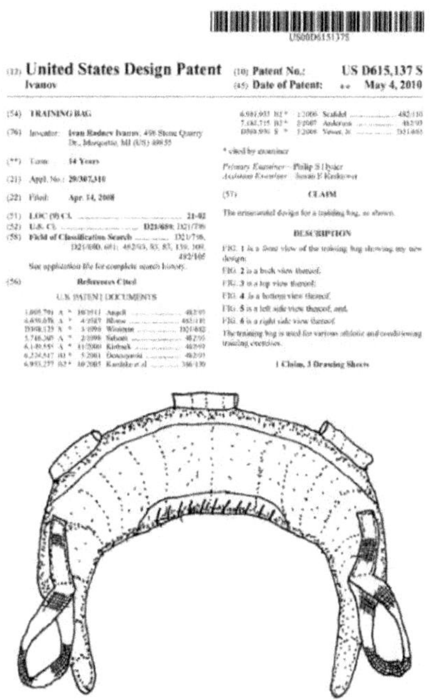

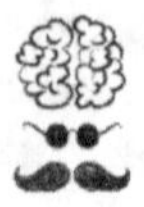

154.

In 2011, fashion brand Abercrombie & Fitch offered a "substantial" amount of money to Michael Sorrentino – aka The Situation from MTV's Jersey Shore – not to use its clothes.

155.

Twin rates show a wide geographical and temporal variation, being extremely low in Asian populations (5-6 in 1,000 births) and higher in Sub-Saharan populations (23 in 1,000 births).

156.

Cândido Godói (CG) is a small town in south Brazil with approximately 6,000 inhabitants, known as the "Twins' Town". According to the Brazilian Ministry of Health, in the period 1994-2006, 2% of the live births in CG were twins, while the average for the whole country is about 1%. However, twinning is not equally distributed throughout the municipality. In 1994, the twinning birth rate in Linha São Pedro, a small district of CG was estimated at 10%. However, the reasons for the higher twinning rate in CG in general, and in Linha São Pedro in particular, are still unclear.

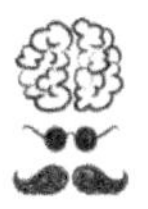

157.

Ever heard of Siddhattha Gotama (aka Siddhārtha Gautama)? He was a philosopher, religious leader, and spiritual teacher, and who lived in ancient India (5th to 4th century BCE). Maybe you know him better under another name, the Buddha.

158.

Da Hong Pao is one of the world's most expensive teas and costs more than 30 times its weight in gold – $1,400 (€1,250) for a gram. It is a rare and expensive strain of oolong tea, grown in the Wuyishan region of southern China and often aged for up to 80 years before sale.

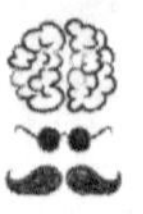

159.

A bear stock market is characterized by falling prices; the opposite of a bull market. The origin of the term "bear market" is not quite clear, but according to some sources, it goes back to the sale of bearskins. In the 1700s, middlemen would sell the skins before they actually had them in hand and then hope that the price would fall and they could purchase them for less. Those traders came to be called bears, or, as described in The Tatler in 1709, someone who "ensures a Real Value upon an Imaginary Thing".

160.

In 2016, scientists proved that riding on some types of roller coaster could be an effective way of removing kidney stones. The report was published in the peer-reviewed Journal of the American Osteopathic Association.

161.

In 2018, a mega planet, almost 13 times bigger than Jupiter, was detected some 20 light-years away from Earth. The planet is not attached to any star and it is the first object of its kind to be discovered.

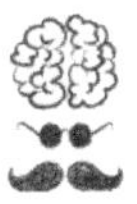

162.

Ralph Henry Baer, born Rudolf Heinrich Baer (1922-2014), was a German-American inventor. Baer is considered "the Father of Video Games" due to his many contributions to games and helped to spark the video game industry in the latter half of the 20th century.

163.

If your definition of "famous" is "notable enough to have a Wikipedia page", then about 1 out of every 10,000 people on Earth are famous today.

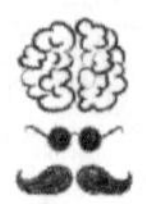

164.

Normally, the efficiency of a drug is tested against a placebo. This should not be construed, however, as proof that the placebo itself is useless. The findings of a 2009 Harvard Medical School placebo study were quite surprising: nearly twice as many people in the trial who knowingly received placebo pills reported experiencing adequate symptom relief, compared to the people receiving no treatment. Nowadays, many people are taking placebos to deal with their health problems and it is working.

165.

According to NASA, one gram of antimatter costs $62.5 trillion (€ 55 trillion).

166.

Blind people are twice as likely to smell something in their dreams as sighted people.

167.

Erramatti Mangamma from Hyderabad, India, currently holds the record for being the oldest living mother at the age of 74 after conceiving through the process of in-vitro fertilisation. She delivered twin baby girls, which also made her the oldest mother to give birth to twins.

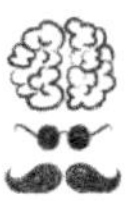

168.

In 1972, Jean Boulet of France piloted an Aérospatiale SA 315B Lama helicopter to an absolute altitude record of 12,440 m (40,814 ft). At that extreme altitude, the engine malfunctioned and Boulet had to land the helicopter by breaking another record: the longest successful autorotation in history.

169.

In 1895, the Croatian city of Šibenik became the first in the world with streetlights powered by alternating current (AC).

170.

In 2018, James Owers booked train tickets for himself and his girlfriend Deena to travel from Edinburgh to Inverness, Scotland. They were able to get Deena's bike on the train, but there was no space for James's bike. He decided to cycle all the way from Edinburgh to Inverness (270 km or 170 miles) and arrived before the train did.

171.

Rocket engines' power is still measured in horsepower.

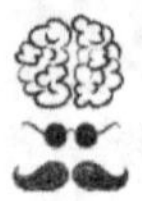

172.

The first touchscreen was designed and put to use in 1973.

173.

When someone takes too much LSD, they may experience terrifying hallucinations, but technically a person cannot take a lethal dose. By the way, experienced meditators and LSD users have remarkably similar brain activity patterns.

174.

If a house or apartment for sale smells of freshly made coffee or toasted bread, it will sell faster due to the so-called Proust effect, which refers to the vivid reliving of events from the past through sensory stimuli.

175.

All of the planets in our Solar System could fit in the distance between Earth and the Moon.

176.

The maximum number of Friday the 13th in a year is three, and the minimum is one.

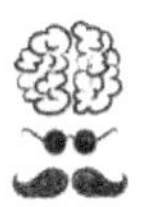

177.

As of this writing, the longest commercial nonstop flight takes almost 19 hours: from Newark, New Jersey (USA), to Singapore: 15,344 km (9,534 mi).

178.

In April 2020, the US Patent and Trademark Office refused two patents where the AI (artificial intelligence) system Dabus was listed as the inventor. It ruled that only "natural persons" could be inventors.

179.

The word "guerrilla" derives from the Spanish resistance to France's invading armies (1808-14). The Spanish uprising forced Emperor Napoleon Bonaparte to deal with a new kind of enemy: The Guerrilla. His troops in Spain had to wage two wars: a conventional one against the Spanish army and the British Expeditionary Force; and an unconventional one against the people themselves.

180.

Lufthansa flights departing from the German airports of Frankfurt and Munich have even numbers. Odd numbers are assigned for trips back to the home base.

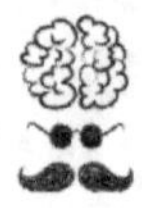

181.

The Game of Thrones TV series is based on George R. R. Martin's fantasy novel series "A Song of Ice and Fire".

182.

Rabindranath Tagore from India was the first non-European author to be awarded the Nobel Prize for Literature, in 1913.

183.

Ancient Rome differed from Greek city-states in allowing freed slaves to become plebeian citizens. After being set free, former Roman slaves were also granted active political freedom, including the right to vote.

184.

According to the security procedures of many air companies, when one of the pilots needs to use the toilet, a flight attendant goes into the cockpit and waits until the pilot returns. This is done to avoid issues such as being locked out of the cockpit if the second pilot suddenly passes out.

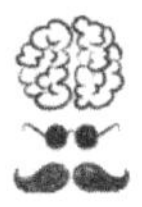

185.

When a young German researcher named Alfred Wegener proposed in 1912 that all of Earth's major continents were once joined in a gigantic landmass (he called it "Pangea") and were slowly moving apart, the overwhelming majority of contemporary scientists laughed at him. The continental drift theory he advocated was universally accepted some 50 years later.

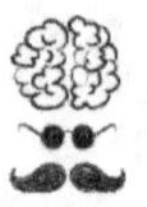

186.

José Gabriel Túpac Amaru (1738-1781) – known as Túpac Amaru II – was the leader of a large Andean uprising against the Spanish in Peru, whose quelling resulted in his death. He turned into a mythical figure in the Peruvian struggle for independence and indigenous rights movement, as well as an inspiration to countless causes worldwide:

- The Peruvian guerrilla faction Túpac Amaru Revolutionary Movement;

- The Tupamaros (aka the National Liberation Movement), an urban guerrilla group in Uruguay;

- The Venezuelan Marxist political party Tupamaro;

- American rapper, Tupac Amaru Shakur (aka 2Pac), was named after him.

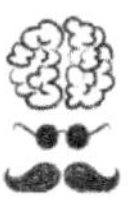

187.

Rosetta was a space probe built by the European Space Agency and launched on 2 March 2004. It carried out a detailed study of comet 67P/Churyumov–Gerasimenko (67P). Its lander module, Philae, made the first soft landing on a comet nucleus on 12 November 2014.

188.

Worldwide, China has the highest number of people without religion (atheists and agnostics) – some 200 million.

189.

Champagne is a French sparkling wine. Many people use the term Champagne as a generic term for sparkling wine, but in Europe and some other countries, it is illegal to label any product Champagne unless it came from the Champagne wine region of France and was produced under the rules of the appellation of controlled origin.

190.

Sir Dick White (1906-1993) is the only person so far to have headed both MI6 and MI5: the British intelligence and counter-intelligence services, respectively.

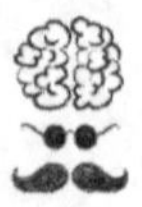

191.

The Kármán line is an effort to define the imaginary border between Earth's atmosphere and outer space. This is crucial for legal and regulatory measures; aircraft and spacecraft fall under different jurisdictions and are subject to different treaties. The Fédération Aéronautique Internationale (World Air Sports Federation), an international standard-setting and record-keeping institution for aeronautics and astronautics, defines the Kármán line as the altitude of 100 km (62 mi) above Earth's mean sea level. Other organizations, however, do not stick to the same definition. For instance, the US Air Force and NASA define the limit to be 80 km (50 mi) above sea level.

192.

80% to 95% of East Asians have dry earwax, whereas the wet variety is abundant in people of African and European ancestry (97% to 100%).

193.

The first Nobel prizes in Chemistry, Literature, Peace, Physics, and Physiology or Medicine were awarded in 1901. The first Swedish laureate was Svante August Arrhenius (1859-1927), for Chemistry in 1903.

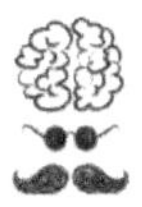

194.

The oldest noble vine in the world still bearing grapes is in Maribor, Slovenia. According to the Guinness Book of Records, it is over 400 years old.

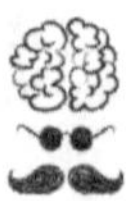

195.

As a part of Champagne production process, secondary fermentation in the bottle causes carbonation and some residue. To remove the residue without losing the carbonation, the bottle neck of each bottle is shock-frozen while the bottle is upside down, the residue is thus captured in the block of ice and extracted. Then some wine is added, and the bottle is sealed again.

196.

According to several studies, sunlight exposure reduces myopia in children.

197.

Ericsson Globe in Stockholm, Sweden, is currently the largest hemispherical building in the world. It has a diameter of 110 m (361 ft) and an inner height of 85 m (279 ft).

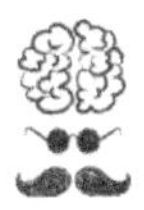

198.

The Boeing 777X is the latest model of the long-range Boeing 777 family from Boeing Commercial Airplanes. As of this writing, it has the largest engine-diameter with a fan diameter of 339 cm (11 ft 1.5 in).

199.

Air weighs about 1.29 grams per litre. Water weighs 1,000 grams per litre. The ratio between them is therefore roughly 1.29:1000, water being approximately 775 times heavier than air.

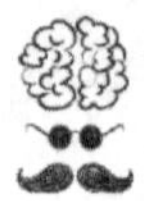

200.

The biggest beer tent at the Munich Oktoberfest, Germany, can accommodate up to 9,991 visitors.

201.

What do the following have in common: Viagra, Slinky, Penicillin, Potato chips, Pacemaker, Microwave ovens, Saccharin (an artificial sweetener), Fireworks, Corn Flakes, LSD as a drug, Ink-Jet printers, Post-it notes, X-Rays? They were all invented by accident.

202.

If spread on the land, all the salt from the oceans would create a layer 150 m (500 ft) high.

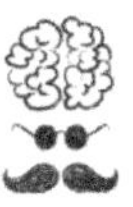

203.

Ginseng is the root of plants in the *genus Panax*, rich in ginsenosides and gintonin. The most popular sorts are the Korean ginseng (*P. ginseng*), the South China ginseng (*P. notoginseng*), and the American ginseng (*P. quinquefolius*). Although ginseng has been used in Eastern Asia's traditional medicine over centuries, modern clinical research is inconclusive about its medical effectiveness. In 2007, the root of an over 300-year-old wild ginseng was sold for the equivalent of $440,000 (€400,000) in China.

204.

Twinings Tea has been using the same logo for 233 years, making it the world's oldest unchanged logo in continuous use, according to the company website.

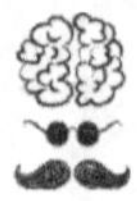

205.

Vegetables in the US state of Alaska can grow humongous. This is because during the summer they are exposed to twenty hours of sunlight each day.

206.

Albert Einstein's brain weighed only 1,230 grams (43 oz), while the average adult male brain weighs about 1,400 grams (49 oz). However, the density of neurons was greater.

207.

The speed record for steam locomotives is 200.4 km/h (124.5 mph). It remains unbroken since 1938.

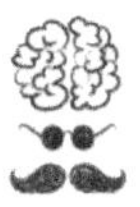

208.

The spaghetti-tree hoax was a report broadcast on April Fools' Day 1957 by the British Broadcasting Company (BBC). BBC's programme Panorama presented a family in southern Switzerland "harvesting" spaghetti from "spaghetti trees". At the time, spaghetti pasta was relatively exotic in the United Kingdom and most Britons were ignorant that it is made from flour. On the following day, numerous viewers contacted the BBC inquiring how to grow their own spaghetti trees.

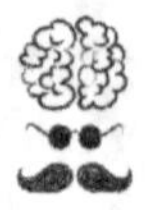

209.

Perovskite ($CaTiO_3$) is the most abundant mineral of Earth's lower mantle [i.e. at a depth of 700-2,900 km (435-1,800 mi)] and accounts for approximately half of Earth's mass.

210.

Prince Rogers Nelson, aka Prince (1958-2016), was a US singer-songwriter, musician, dancer, actor, and filmmaker. In 1993, during a contractual dispute with Warner Bros, Prince changed his name to an unpronounceable symbol and began creating new albums at a much faster rate. This way, he managed to quickly meet the contractually required quota and release himself from further obligations to Warner Bros.

211.

The first song sung in space was "Happy Birthday to You", by the crew of Apollo IX on 8 March 1969.

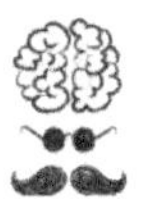

212.

Newcastle upon Tyne, commonly known as Newcastle, is a city in northeast England. Historically, Newcastle's third major export after coal and beer was urine (for dye-making).

213.

Logistics or Logistics Art Project is a 2012 experimental art film. Created by Erika Magnusson and Daniel Andersson, it is the longest film ever made, with an overall duration of 35 days and 17 hours.

214.

There are 19 ingredients in McDonald's French fries. One of them is dextrose – a natural form of sugar that gives the fries their perfect golden colour.

215.

Cummingtonite is a mineral named after the town of Cummington, Massachusetts (USA). Its weird name laid the foundation for a joke known especially amongst geologists and chemists.

216.

It takes up to one hour for a snowflake to fall to the ground from a cloud.

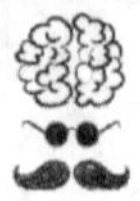

217.

Rubber bands last longer when refrigerated.

218.

An apple would keep you awake better than a cup of coffee. Apples contain no caffeine, but instead have about 14 grams (half an ounce) of natural sugars. These sugars elicit a similar response to caffeine and, what is more important, vitamins from the fruit are released gradually throughout the body, making you feel more awake. There is no peak of energy, but the results vanish as slowly as they started.

219.

In the UK, sausages were called bangers during WWI. Due to meat shortages, sausages contained so much water that they often exploded when fried.

220.

Bagpipes are mentioned in the Bible.

221.

The combined mass of all the asteroids in the Solar System is less than that of Earth's Moon.

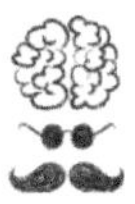

222.

The beard of Hans N. Langseth (1846-1927) measured 5.33 m (17 ft 6 in) at the time of his burial at Kensett, Iowa (USA).

223.

In a 2008 study, a team at the University of British Columbia and Harvard Business School found that spending as little as $5 a day on someone else could significantly boost happiness, more than spending the money on yourself.

224.

Tired people are better at solving problems that require creativity.

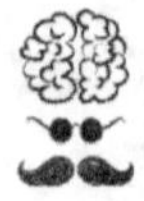

225.

Worldwide, more than one-third of people have never seen snow.

226.

Until late 2017, it was impossible to block Mark Zuckerberg on Facebook.

227.

Sir Edmund Percival Hillary (1919-2008) was a New Zealand explorer and climber. On 29 May 1953, Hillary and his companion Tenzing Norgay, a Sherpa mountaineer, became the first people confirmed to have reached the summit of Mount Everest. Obscure fact: because of his hobby, Hillary was often referred to as "the most famous beekeeper in the world".

228.

Printer paper can be recycled on average five to seven times. Paper is normally made up of long fibres, but every time it is recycled, those fibres get shorter, making it harder to be recycled further. That is why shredders are not friends of paper for recycling.

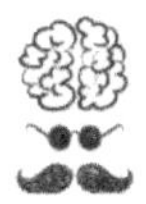

229.

As of 2015, there were 15,372 golf courses in the USA. This is 45% of all golf courses in the entire world.

230.

The Gate Tower Building is a 16-floor office building in Osaka, Japan. It is remarkable for the highway that passes through the building.

231.

Many schools worldwide use meditation and yoga instead of detention for undisciplined students.

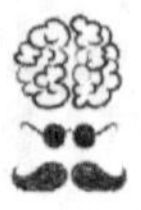

232.

A Portuguese aristocrat, Luis Carlos de Noronha Cabral da Camara, left his fortune to 70 total strangers. When he was writing his will, he asked a notary for a copy of the Lisbon phone book and picked names at random. The lucky ones were contacted out of the blue after his death to be told that da Camara had made them his beneficiaries.

233.

Air Transat Flight 236 was a flight from Toronto, Canada, to Lisbon, Portugal, which lost all engine power while cruising over the Atlantic Ocean on 24 August 2001. The Airbus A330 remained without fuel due to a leak caused by poor maintenance. Captain Robert Piché, an accomplished glider pilot, and First Officer Dirk de Jager completed a successful emergency landing in the Azores, saving all 306 people (293 passengers and 13 crew) on board. They glided over 120 km (75 mi) which remains a record glide length for a commercial aircraft. Media broadly declared the captain a hero, while not missing the opportunity to disclose that he had served time in prison for drug smuggling in the 1980s.

234.

On most airplane safety instructions cards, the only word visible on the pictograms is "Exit".

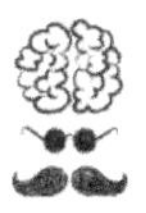

235.

In 1947, Norwegian explorer and writer, Thor Heyerdahl, led the Kon-Tiki expedition – a raft journey across the Pacific Ocean from South America to the Polynesian islands. Heyerdahl proved that peoples from South America could have reached and settled in Polynesia in thousands of years ago by using only the materials and technologies available at the time. Kon-Tiki is also the title of Heyerdahl's book, the Oscar-winning 1950 documentary film describing his adventures, and the 2012 film nominated for Oscar.

236.

If you sign a testimony at the beginning of the document, you are more honest than if you sign it at the end.

242.

Martin Creed's Work No. 227 consists of an empty room with lights on a time switch, going on and off every five seconds. British modern and contemporary art gallery, Tate, bought the work for its permanent collection, saying it was "arguably one of Martin Creed's most famous works".

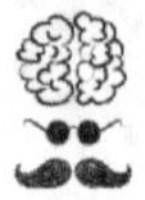

237.

Bananas were first produced in Iceland in 1941. Using cheap geothermal energy to heat the greenhouses and cheap electricity to provide illumination during the darkest months made it possible to grow bananas in the middle of the North Atlantic.

238.

Ciabatta bread was invented in 1982.

239.

Diamond is the gem with the simplest chemical composition.

240.

Water accounts for only 0.02% of the total mass of our planet.

241.

Gummy bears can be used as rocket fuel.

CHAPTER IV

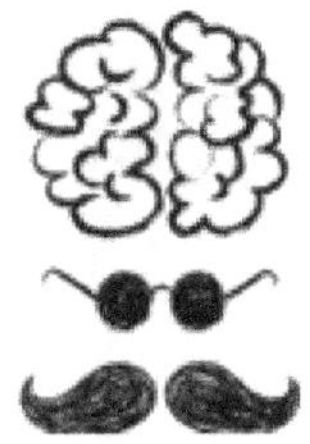

SPORTS

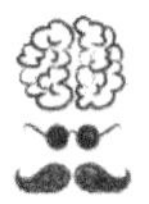

243.

In the USA, slam-dunking was banned in NCAA (college) basketball in the period 1967-76. The ban was dubbed the "Lew Alcindor Rule" after the UCLA star and slam dunk king who would later become Kareem Abdul-Jabbar.

244.

Iceland is the only remaining Nordic country to outlaw boxing. Boxing was initially made illegal because residents directly attributed an increase in violent crimes to the sport's rise in popularity during the 1930s and 1940s. As a direct response to boxing's ban, alternative martial arts like judo, karate, MMA, and taekwondo have gained popularity in the country.

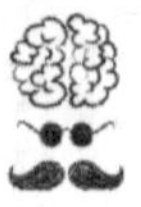

245.

Facing unbearable heat, Qatar has started to air-condition open-air football stadiums. Henceforth in this book, facts about "football" refer to the sport popular in the USA under the name "soccer".

246.

In football, a red card is shown by the referee to signal that a player must be sent off. This player has to leave the field of play without delay and cannot be replaced by a substitute, compelling their team to play with one player less. If a team's goalkeeper receives a red card, another player is required to assume goalkeeping duties, so teams will usually substitute another goalkeeper for an outfield player if they still have substitutes available. While rare, there have been occasions when players received red cards for attacking teammates.

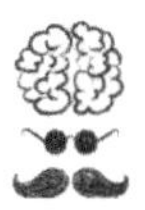

247.

The French Lyon Foundation broke the world record for the longest football match in 2019. The game went on for 68 hours and finished 399:369. 807 participants from sixty different countries took part, with teams taking turns playing five-a-side games for three days and two nights non-stop.

248.

A qualifying match for the 2002 FIFA World Cup between the national football (soccer) teams of Australia and American Samoa ended with a whopping result of 31:0.

249.

In boxing, neither fighters nor crowd know the score before the end of the match.

250.

The largest number of penalties in an official football (soccer) match is 48. It happened in 2005, when Namibian KK Palace beat Civics 17:16. However, the highest score in a penalty shoot-out was achieved in the 1988 Argentine Championship, when Argentinos Juniors beat Racing Club 20:19 after 44 penalties.

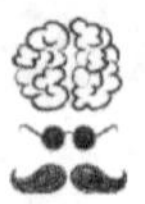

251.

Roberto Martin Antonio Bonilla (born in 1963) is a former baseball player in the US major leagues from 1986 to 2001. From 1992 to 1994, Bonilla was the highest-paid sportsperson in the league, earning more than $6 million per year. He will also be remembered as the baseball player who received almost $30 million for not playing. Let me explain: New York Mets released Bonilla before the 2000 season while still owing him $5.9 million for the final year of his contract. Instead of paying the lump sum, the team agreed to make 25 annual payments of $1.2 million each in the period 2009-2035.

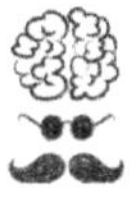

252.

In a 1975 Asia Cup semi-final football game, North Korea and Hong Kong finished 3:3 after extra time. They needed 28 penalties to decide the winner: North Korea.

253.

In late-2019, Swiss tennis legend Roger Federer became the first living person to be featured on a Swiss coin (20-franc silver coin) as "a perfect ambassador" for the country.

254.

Athletes perform better if their main rival participates in the competition.

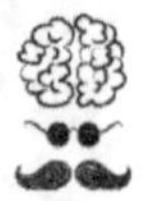

255.

In chess, the queen was originally the counsellor or prime minister or vizier. Initially its only move was one square diagonally. Around 1300 CE, its move was enhanced to allow it to jump two squares diagonally (onto a same-coloured square) for its first move. The first surviving mention of this piece as a queen or similar was "regina" in the Einsiedeln Poem, written in Latin around 997 CE and preserved in a monastery in Einsiedeln, Switzerland.

256.

Jerome Boateng and Kevin-Prince Boateng are paternal half-brothers and professional football players. During the 2010 World Cup, they were the first set of brothers to take the field together representing opposing national teams.

257.

Sumo wrestlers throw salt into the ring prior to the match as a tribute to the spirits.

258.

In boxing, the wearing of a beard is prohibited.

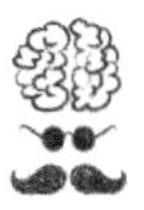

259.

In US baseball, the Cincinnati Red Stockings of 1869 were the first professional team, with ten salaried players.

260.

On 11 September 1875, two women's teams competed in Springfield, Illinois (USA). Dubbed the Blondes and the Brunettes, the players became the first known women to be paid for playing baseball.

261.

In baseball, a hitting streak is the number of consecutive official games in which a player has at least one base hit. The Major League Baseball record remains unbroken since 1941, set by Joe DiMaggio with 56 consecutive games.

262.

The first written records of the ancient Olympic Games date to 776 BCE, when a cook named Coroebus became the first Olympic champion by winning the only event – a 192-metre footrace called the "stade". By the way, the word we use today to designate a "stadium" derives from "stade".

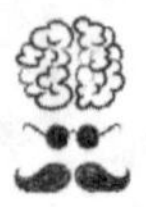

263.

The 1904 Summer Olympics took place in St. Louis, Missouri (USA). It was the first time that the Olympic Games were organised outside Europe. Two athletes achieved remarkable feats: the US gymnast, George Eyser, won six medals even though his left leg was made of wood, and Frank Kugler won four medals in freestyle wrestling, weightlifting, and tug of war, making him the only sportsperson to win a medal in three different disciplines at the same Olympic Games.

264.

Town planning used to be an Olympic sport in the period 1928-1948.

265.

Ian Millar, CM (born 1947) is a Canadian Equestrian Team athlete for show jumping. He is a two-time winner of the Show Jumping World Cup and an Olympic silver medallist. He holds the record for the most Olympic appearances by any athlete in any sport: ten.

CHAPTER V

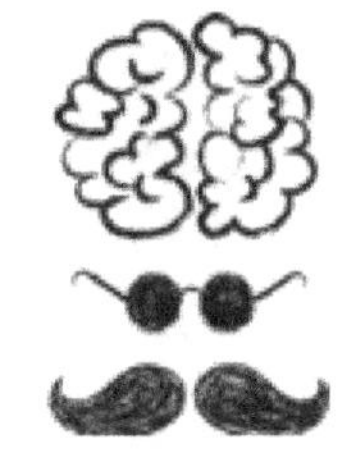

ANIMALS

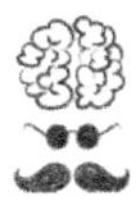

266.

Tarantulas can swim or rather walk on water.

267.

Beavers have orange teeth that contain iron, while other rodents have magnesium in their tooth enamel.

268.

Flamingos can drink boiling water.

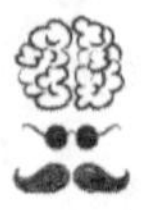

269.

Ferrets are among the top 15 most popular pets in the USA. However, they are illegal to own in California and Hawaii.

270.

Cattle have many more blood types than humans do, making blood transfusion a real challenge. In contrast, cats only have two blood types.

271.

Cat owners are more likely to leave money to their pets in their wills than dog owners are.

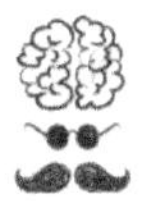

272.

Flamingos and many other birds can sleep standing on one leg.

273.

Australian lizard, the thorny devil (*Moloch horridus*), can sip water from sand through its feet and back. It uses its entire skin as a web of drinking straws to soak up water from soggy sand.

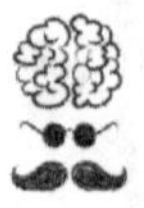

274.

In 2019, a Russian farm provided its dairy cows with virtual reality (VR) headsets that were expected to reduce cows' anxiety. The VR systems were adapted for the cows and projected a "summer field simulation".

275.

For many commercial beekeepers in the USA, most of the revenue now comes from pollinating almonds. Selling honey is not as lucrative as renting their hives to huge farms in California's Central Valley, which provides 80% of the world's almond supply.

276.

Bees can detect explosives and can solve basic algebra problems.

277.

Three-toed sloths spend most of their lives in the trees. They descend to the ground only once a week. To defecate.

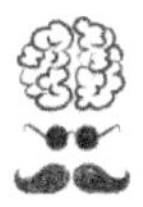

278.

Although they spend most of their time in the trees, sloths are surprisingly good swimmers – they can swim through water three times faster than they can move on the ground.

279.

Sloths can hold their breath for up to 40 minutes; dolphins – only 10 minutes.

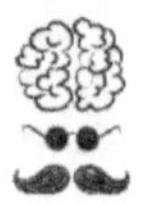

280.

Leafcutter ants can lift up to 50 times their own body weight, which is beneficial since they survive by foraging for large leaves. However, what is even more impressive is that they carry these heavy loads using only their jaws.

281.

In 2012, scientists named a prehistoric woodpecker after South Africa's first black president, Nelson Mandela (*Australopicus nelsonmandelai*).

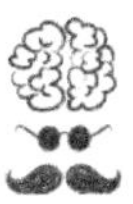

282.

Horseshoe crab blood is a valuable resource to the medical research. Blue in colour, it can identify bacterial contamination in small quantities. Horseshoe crab blood contains a special amebocyte that is separated and then used in food testing.

283.

There are no green mammals. While sloths can sometimes look green, this is due to the algae growing on their fur.

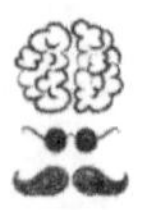

284.

Crows and ravens are the only North American bird species that are completely black in colour. And yes, although they look very similar, ravens (on the left) and crows (on the right) are two separate species.

285.

On a tiny island near Warrnambool, Australia, Maremma Sheepdogs are guarding Little Penguins, the smallest penguin species. Almost extinct in the early 2000s, the birds are now thriving and breeding, as predation losses from foxes – their chief killers – have ceased since the introduction of the dogs. The world-first project was so successful it attracted interest from all over the world and, in 2015, inspired a family film, Oddball.

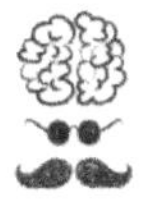

286.

An oologist is someone who studies bird eggs.

287.

A 2018 research confirmed that the bonnethead shark is the first omnivore shark. It inhabits the shallow, coastal areas along the USA's Pacific and Atlantic coast. These areas have plenty of seagrass, which, together with shrimps and crabs, comprise this shark's food of choice.

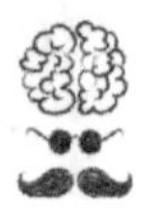

288.

Military police patrol the streets of the Brazilian island of Marajo mounted on gigantic water buffaloes.

289.

Seabirds have no problem drinking sea water. The salt they take in is absorbed and moves through their bloodstream into a pair of salt glands above the eyes. The densely salty fluid is then excreted from the nostrils.

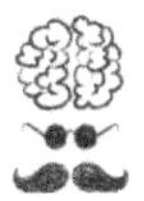

290.

The Wolong Natural Nature Reserve in Sichuan Province, China, offers a job where you can dress up as a panda to play with real panda cubs.

291.

Deinococcus radiodurans is a bacterium famous for its high resistance to extreme radiation and oxidants. It is notable for its ability to biosynthesize gold nanoparticles (AuNPs). AuNPs have found a wide range of applications in electronics, biomedical engineering, and chemistry owing to their exceptional opto-electrical properties.

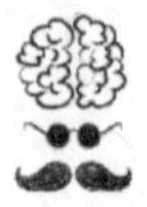

292.

There have been many unusual eBay listings. While by far not the most bizarre, two of them have led to scientific discoveries. In September 2006, a sea urchin turned out to be a new species, later given the name *Coelopleurus exquisitus*. In August 2008, Dr Richard Harrington, Vice President of the UK Royal Entomological Society, announced that a fossilized aphid he had bought for £20 ($27 or €23) from a seller in Lithuania proved to be a previously unknown species. It was named *Mindarus harringtoni* after Dr Harrington. He wanted to name it *Mindarus ebayi*, but this name was disallowed for not being "scientific enough". The 45-million-year-old aphid, preserved in a piece of Baltic amber, is now housed in the Natural History Museum in London, UK.

293.

Only five countries worldwide have polar bears: Russia, the United States, Denmark (Greenland), Norway, and Canada.

294.

Lobsters are really close to being immortal: they show no visible signs of ageing, no deterioration of health, and no slowdown in metabolism.

295.

Pan Pan (1985-2016) was a male giant panda who lived in the Giant Panda Protection and Research Centre in Chengdu, China. At the time of his demise, he was the oldest male giant panda in captivity. He is notable to have about 150 descendants – close to 30% of the world's captive-bred panda population.

296.

If you put a ladybug on a sheet of paper and start drawing a line, the insect will follow the line. There are plenty of interesting videos online.

297.

In 2016, a joint US-Canadian study confirmed that the striped shore crab, *Pachygrapsus crassipes*, is sensitive to human antidepressant drugs, such as Prozac.

298.

In building their nests, many birds use spider webbing as a "glue" to bind together other nesting materials, such as straw, twigs, roots, and lichens. Sticky spider silk is also important as an adhesive to attach nests securely to leaves, twigs, and branches.

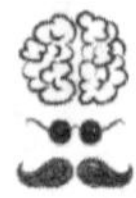

299.

The orang-utan is the only ape in Asia. The male orang-utan is the largest tree mammal in the world.

300.

In 2011, it was revealed that elephants have six toes (including a pseudo toe) on each foot. We have to note that not every toe has a corresponding toenail.

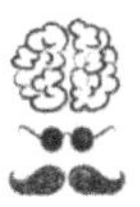

301.

Elephants can "hear" through their feet. They are capable of the so-called seismic communication. Elephants' sensitive feet capture the slightest vibration, be it the steps of humans, elephants or other animals, distant elephant alarm cries, mating calls, and navigation instructions to the herd.

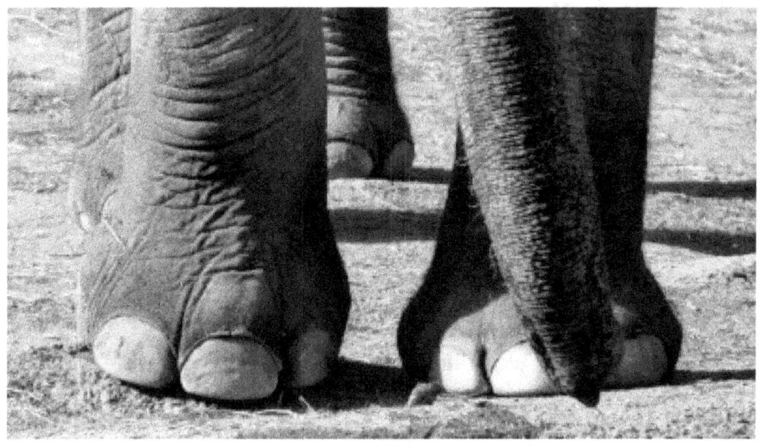

302.

Often compared to an air conditioner, elephants' ears have large blood vessels that are visible from the back of the ear. Blood circulates through those vessels and cools down, then continues cooling down the rest of their bodies.

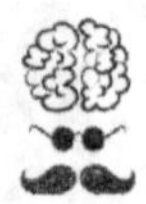

303.

It may sound strange, but banana peels are actually an effective treatment for mosquito bites (by simply rubbing the fleshy side down). This is due to the natural oils found within the banana's skin.

304.

Many bird species move their upper jaw a bit, but parrots move it the most. Parrots are unique in being able to move their upper beak independently and upward in relation to the lower beak.

305.

According to a study from 2008, domestic cattle and deer align their body axes roughly in the north-south direction when grazing or taking a nap.

306.

The weight of the baby koala at the time of its birth is around 1 gram.

307.

On average, scientists worldwide discover dozens of new species every day.

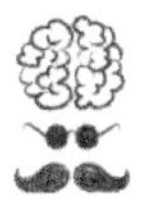

308.

African giant pouched rats have poor vision but an extraordinary sense of smell. They are very efficient in discovering hidden landmines by sniffing out the explosive TNT. One rat can search 200 m² (over 2,100 sq. ft) in 20 minutes, an area that could take a human up to four days. And as if these capabilities were not enough, the rats can also be trained to successfully detect tuberculosis.

309.

The boa constrictor's common name and scientific name are exactly the same.

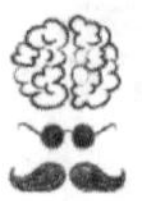

310.

The grey fox (*Urocyon cinereoargenteus*) is widespread throughout North America and Central America. It is unique in that it is a skilled tree climber. Grey foxes can climb trees that are straight up to escape their predators but they also climb to take a nap in a sunny location, and have been known to hide or sleep in hawk and owl nests.

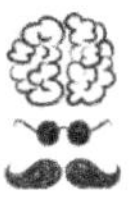

311.

Cartilaginous fish (with skeleton made of cartilage, rather than bone), such as sharks and rays, do not have swim bladders. Some of the species have adapted to control their depth only by swimming (using dynamic lift); others stockpile fats with lesser density than seawater to achieve a neutral buoyancy, which does not change with depth.

312.

The bony-eared assfish (*Acanthonus armatus*) holds the record for the smallest brain-to-body weight ratio of all vertebrates.

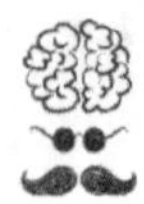

313.

Tuataras are reptiles endemic to New Zealand. Although bearing a resemblance to lizards, tuataras belong to a distinct lineage, the order Rhynchocephalia. They are unique for having two rows of teeth in the upper jaw overlapping one row on the lower jaw. Tuataras also possess a photoreceptive eye, the third eye, which plays role in setting circadian and seasonal cycles. As if they were not strange enough, male tuataras have no penis at all.

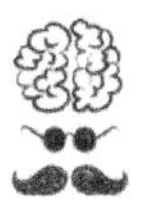

314.

Monarch butterflies (*Danaus plexippus*) and dragonflies (*Pantala flavescens*) are the two insects capable of the longest distance travel on annual basis: 4,000 km (2,500 mi) and 7,000 km (4,400 mi), respectively.

315.

Several bat species are the main pollinators of African baobab. The large flowers are well-suited to bat pollination because they are large enough to support a bat while it sucks nectar.

316.

Human beings are the only species among primates to have chins. Archaeologists can use the absence of a chin to separate Neanderthals from modern humans.

317.

The European mole (*Talpa europaea*) can be found throughout Europe, but not in Norway, nor in island countries such as Northern Ireland and the Republic of Ireland, Malta, and Cyprus.

CHAPTER VI

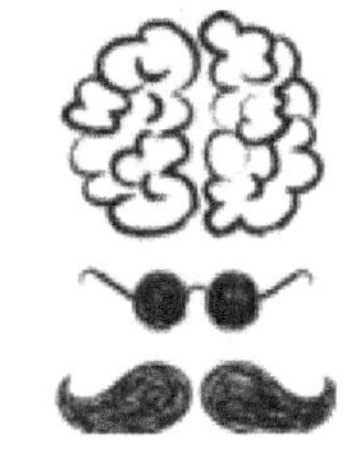

LANGUAGE

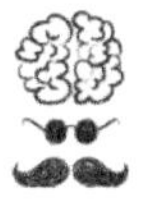

318.

The official French word for "fake news" is "infox".

319.

The Japanese equivalent of goodbye – sayonara – means literally "if it must be so".

320.

All odd numbers have the letter "e" inside their name.

321.

The name "Sahara" is derived from a dialectal Arabic word for, unsurprisingly, "desert".

322.

"Ciao" is Italy's most common and simple greeting word. It derives from an old Venetian dialect word meaning slave: "sciao" ("schiavo" in standard Italian). Sciao was used as a greeting word meaning "I am your slave" i.e. "I am at your service".

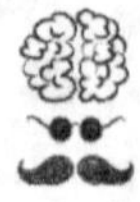

323.

The small dot on a lowercase letter i or j is called a tittle or superscript dot.

324.

According to the dictionary by Merriam-Webster, there are three ways to reference more than one octopus: octopi, octopuses, and octopodes. These three forms are all correct.

325.

The Turkish language has three words for "red": "kırmızı", "al", and "kızıl". Additionally, Turkish has two words for "white" ("beyaz" and "ak") and two for "black" ("siyah" and "kara"). Likewise, in Irish there are two words for "green": "glas" denotes the green colour of grass, while "uaine" describes artificial greens. Multiple words for "red" are found in Irish and Scottish Gaelic ("dearg" for light, bright red, and "rua" or "ruadh" respectively for dark and brownish red). Hungarian also has two words

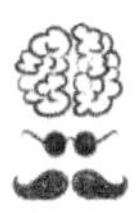

for "red": "piros" and "vörös". Counter-intuitively, they are both interchangeable in some cases and not in others. For instance, blood can be either, but wine is always "vörös".

326.

The language you speak may influence how you perceive colours, according to a 2007 research of Massachusetts Institute of Technology in Cambridge, USA. Russian speakers, who use separate words for light and dark blue, are indeed better at discriminating between the two, suggesting that they really perceive them as different colours. Russian people split what the English language regards as "blue" into two distinctive colours, named "goluboy" (light blue) and "siniy" (dark blue). Researchers showed to Russian and English speakers sets of three blue squares – two of which were identical shades with a third "odd one out". The volunteers had to pick out the identical squares. Russian speakers were much quicker when the two shades straddled the limit between "goluboy" and "siniy".

327.

Ancient Japanese did not make distinction between green and blue. Still today, the green traffic light in Japan is described using the same word for blue, "aoi".

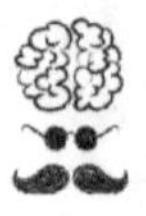

328.

Inuktitut is a language spoken by some 65,000 people throughout Greenland, Canada, Alaska (USA), and Siberia (Russia). It is a written language without an alphabet, but an abugida. Whereas an alphabet utilizes a symbol to represent each of the letters that make up a particular language, an abugida only uses symbols to represent consonant letters, and the orientation of such symbols determines which vowels are to follow. Inuktitut is just one of multiple languages that use an abugida system worldwide. The list includes, among many others: Bengali, Burmese, Ethiopic, Javanese, Khmer, Tamil, Telugu, Thai, and Tibetan.

i	u	a	h
pi	pu	pa	p
ti	tu	ta	t
ki	ku	ka	k
gi	gu	ga	g
mi	mu	ma	m
ni	nu	na	n
si	su	sa	s
li	lu	la	l
ji	ju	ja	j
vi	vu	va	v
ri	ru	ra	r
qi	qu	qa	q
ngi	ngu	nga	ng
nngi	nngu	nnga	nng
ti	tu	ta	ł

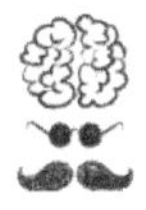

329.

The Pirahã is an isolated tribe in Brazil's Amazon region whose language has no colour words. It is one of the few cultures that can only distinguish between light and dark. They use descriptive phrases such as "(like) blood" for "red". Furthermore, there is no grammatical distinction between singular and plural, even in pronouns.

330.

Linear B, the ancient Mycenaean Greek script, was deciphered by an amateur: Michael George Francis Ventris (1922-1956). Ventris had tried to decode it as a personal dare since his school years.

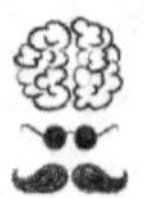

331.

"Mayday" is an emergency word used internationally as a distress signal in voice-procedure radio communications. Not related to the holiday May Day, it derives from the French "m'aider" ("help me"), a shortened form of "venez m'aider" ("come and help me"). Before "mayday", SOS was the Morse code equivalent of distress call.

332.

Baghdad means "bestowed by God" in Middle Persian language.

333.

The term "bankruptcy" derives from the Italian phrase "banca rotta". When merchants and money dealers on the Ponte Vecchio bridge in Florence, Italy, could not pay their debts, their table/bench (banca) was physically broken (rotta).

334.

The name of Cyprus has unknown etymology. What is clear, however, is that the Latin word for copper originated from the phrase "aes Cyprium" ("metal of Cyprus"), later shortened to "Cuprum".

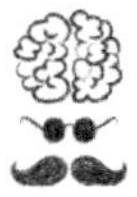

335.

"Bidet" is a French word for "pony", and in 15th-century French, "bider" used to mean "to trot".

336.

Pinocchio is derived from an old Italian word for "pine nut".

337.

A mixologist is a fancy way to say bartender trained to prepare cocktails.

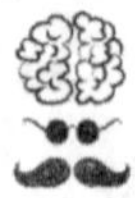

338.

Tiramisu is a coffee-flavoured Italian dessert. Its name derives from Italian, meaning "pick me up" or "cheer me up".

339.

Some Antarctic and sub-Antarctic islands have weird names: Disappointment Island, Fabulous Island, Masked Island, Shag Rock, and Sugar Loaf Rocks.

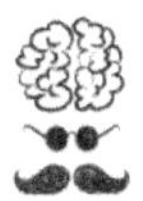

340.

Booby-trap spelled backwards is "partyboob".

341.

The term wypipologist is used by some to humorously describe someone who studies wypipo, aka "white people".

342.

The oldest binary language was invented in China, in the 9th century BCE.

343.

When people use a foreign language in the decision-making process, their decisions tend to be less biased, more analytic, and more systematic, because the foreign language provides psychological distance.

CHAPTER VII

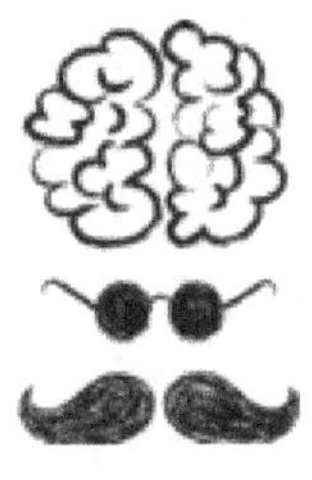

CLIMATE CHANGE

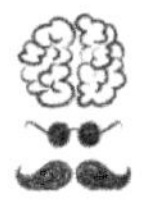

344.

Italy was the first country to make climate change lessons compulsory for all children from 2020.

345.

In 2019, the roofs of 316 bus stops were covered in plants as a gift to honeybees by the city of Utrecht, The Netherlands. Plants support the city's biodiversity, such as honeybees and bumblebees, and also capture fine dust particles and store rainwater.

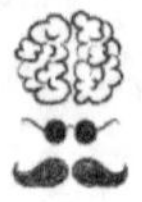

346.

Planting trees reduces crime. According to a 2012 study published in the US journal "Landscape and Urban Planning", it was observed in the neighbourhoods of Baltimore, Maryland, that a 10% increase in tree cover yielded at least a 12% decrease in crime. The researchers controlled for socioeconomic factors, like the fact that wealthier neighbourhoods tend to have leafier lanes. Yet the more-trees/less-crime relation still held.

347.

"Plogging" combines jogging with picking up trash. It started in Sweden in 2015 and rapidly spread to other countries.

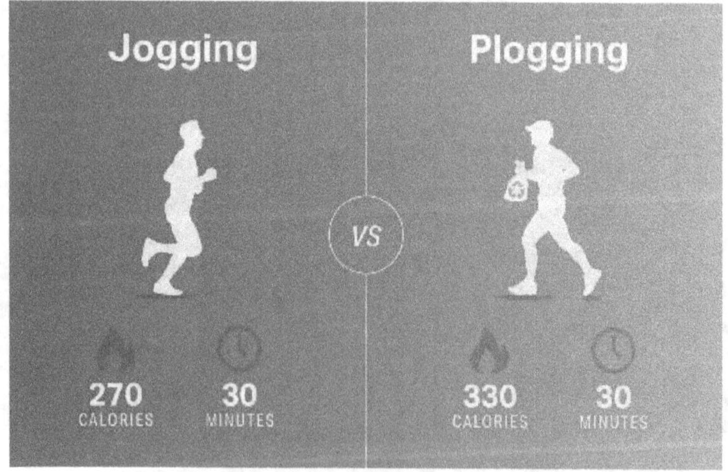

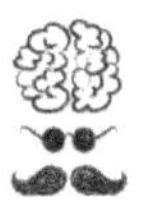

348.

Since 2019, commuters who use public transport in Rome, Italy, can exchange their used plastic bottles for metro or bus tickets. People can simply insert plastic bottles in the machine to receive the ticket on their smartphones through an app.

349.

In 2019, several shops in the Czech Republic introduced shampoo and shower gel filling machines. Customers can now re-use their empty bottles and do not have to buy a new plastic bottle every time.

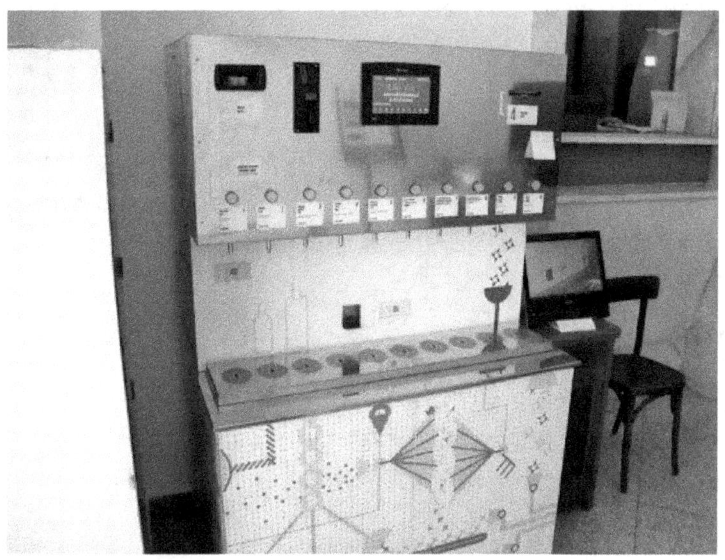

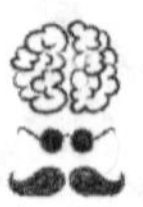

350.

In certain places in the USA, farmers are still being paid by the government to not grow crops. The long-term goal of the Conservation Reserve Program is to re-establish valuable land cover in order to help improve water quality, prevent soil erosion, and reduce loss of wildlife habitat.

351.

According to the Center for Climate, Health, and the Global Environment at Harvard University, USA, high temperatures and heatwaves negatively influence our cognitive speed and memory.

352.

In the 1960s, the electric charge released by radiation from Soviet and US atomic tests led to increased rainfall on the Shetland Islands, Scotland.

353.

Plastic Whale is a Dutch company that provides boat trips down Amsterdam's and Rotterdam's canals for tourists to remove plastic from the water while sightseeing.

CHAPTER VIII

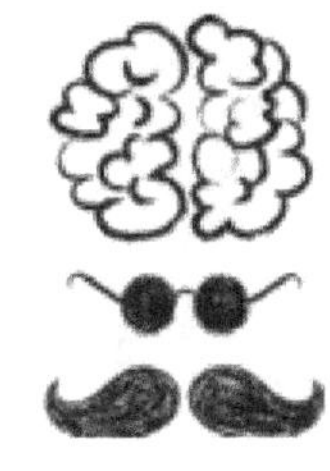

COUNTRIES

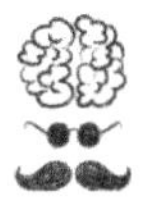

354.

Chad and Romania have identical national flags.

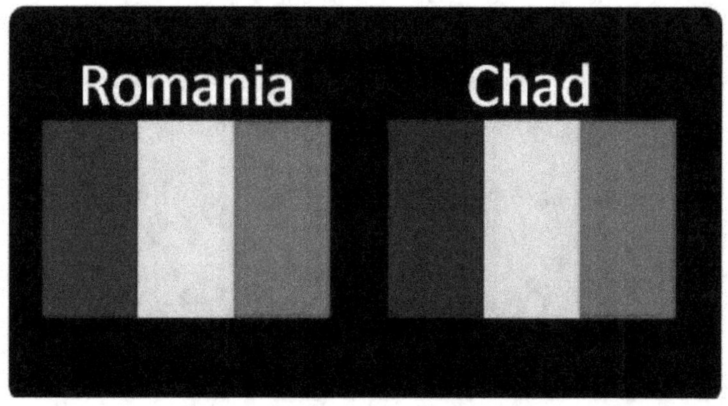

355.

The Netherlands exports more soy sauce than Japan. These two countries are respectively the second and third largest soy sauce exporters after China.

356.

A non-citizen can enlist in the Armed Forces of the United States of America. However, federal law prohibits non-citizens from becoming commissioned or warrant officers.

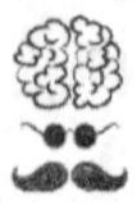

357.

Monaco has an area of only 2 km2 (0.78 sq. mi), making it the second-smallest country in the world after the Vatican City. Its population as of 2018 is 38,682. With 19,009 inhabitants per square kilometre (49,230/sq. mi), it is the most densely populated sovereign state in the world.

358.

In 2014, the Jain pilgrimage destination of Palitana City in the Indian state of Gujarat became the first city in the world to be legally vegetarian. It made illegal the buying and selling of meat, fish, and eggs, along with related activities, such as fishing and penning "food animals".

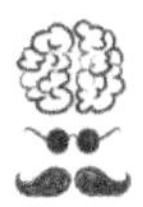

359.

The board game, Monopoly, used to be illegal in Cuba.

360.

The youngest person to have travelled to all sovereign countries is Alexis Alford. In 2019, she visited the last one at the age of 21.

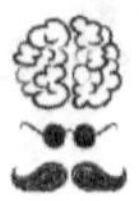

361.

In the Battle of Myeongnyang, on 26 October 1597, a Korean Navy fleet of only 13 ships, led by Admiral Yi Sunsin, fought a Japanese naval force comprising over 130 warships. Korean Admiral Yi held this "last stand" battle against the Japanese Navy and emerged victorious.

362.

Greenland, an autonomous country within the Danish Kingdom, while also being the world's largest island (Australia is larger, but is technically a continent), has a population of only 56,000.

363.

Heidi Gannon was born in Welshpool, Wales, in 1976. Her sister Jo Baines was delivered across the border in Shrewsbury, England, almost two hours later. They are considered the first pair of twins to be born in different countries.

364.

As of today, the ruler of Japan is the only head of state worldwide with the title of "emperor". The Imperial House of Japan is the oldest uninterrupted monarchical house in the world.

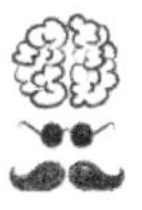

365.

Dahala Khagrabari was an Indian enclave, part of the State of West Bengal. This was a tiny enclave of India within a piece of Bangladesh within an enclave of India within Bangladesh, making it the only third-order enclave (or counter-counter enclave) in the world until 2015, when it was ceded to Bangladesh.

366.

The Øresund (Öresund) Bridge connects the Swedish city of Malmö with the capital of Denmark, Copenhagen. The crossing of the Öresund Strait starts with a combined railway and motorway bridge that extends 8 km (5 mi) from Swedish coast to an artificial island in the middle of the sea. From there, passengers continue their journey under the sea, in the 4-km (2.5-mi) Drogden Tunnel.

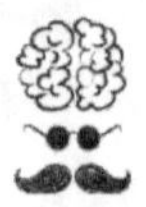

367.

US Highway 550 in Colorado is dubbed the Million Dollar Highway because its roadbed was constructed using low-grade gold ore.

368.

In 1381, Chelmsford was the capital of England for a week. Chelmsford was seriously implicated in the Peasants' Revolt of 1381, and Richard II moved on to the town after crushing the rebellion in London.

369.

Originally, people on the Japanese island of Okinawa drove on the left-hand side of the road, the same as the rest of Japan. However, after the defeat of Japan in World War II, the prefecture went under the control of the United States and in 1945 was made to drive on the right. Okinawa returned to Japanese control in 1972 and changed back to driving on the left in 1978. It is one of very few places to have changed from right- to left-traffic in the late twentieth century or to change the directionality of traffic twice.

370.

Over 10% of the population of South Korea are Catholic.

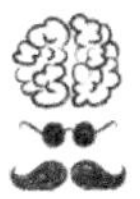

371.

Brought to Japan by a Jesuit missionary, an African slave named Yasuke eventually ended up serving the famous warlord, Oda Nobunaga. He was dubbed the first and only black samurai.

372.

Three out of four ATMs in Japan will not accept foreign bankcards.

373.

Still common today, Japanese adult adoption is a centuries-old practice of legally and socially accepting an unrelated adult into a family. It was developed as a mechanism for families to extend their family name, estate, and ancestry without relying on bloodlines only.

374.

In North Korea, blue jeans are considered bad taste or even illegal. They are thought to symbolise American Imperialism.

375.

One third of the population in Korea is named either Kim or Lee.

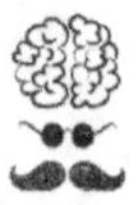

376.

There is no official army in the tiny landlocked country of Andorra (population 85,000), which is protected by France and Spain. However, in case of emergency, all men between the ages of 21 and 60 are required by law to serve and defend. For this reason, by law the male head of each family in Andorra is required to own a gun in case of attack.

377.

The local government in the South Korean capital, Seoul, aims to tackle loneliness and dementia in the rapidly ageing country by organising daytime discos for 65+-year-old seniors.

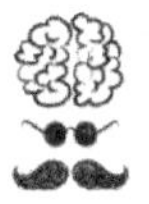

378.

One of the most bizarre complexes of enclaves and exclaves in the world is the Belgian town of Baarle-Hertog. It consists of 24 non-contiguous plots of land, mostly surrounded by the Netherlands. Many houses straddle the border and are simultaneously located in both countries. Each building has to pay taxes in the country where its front door is located. That is why some shops and businesses repeatedly move their front doors some metres if that is profitable for the taxes.

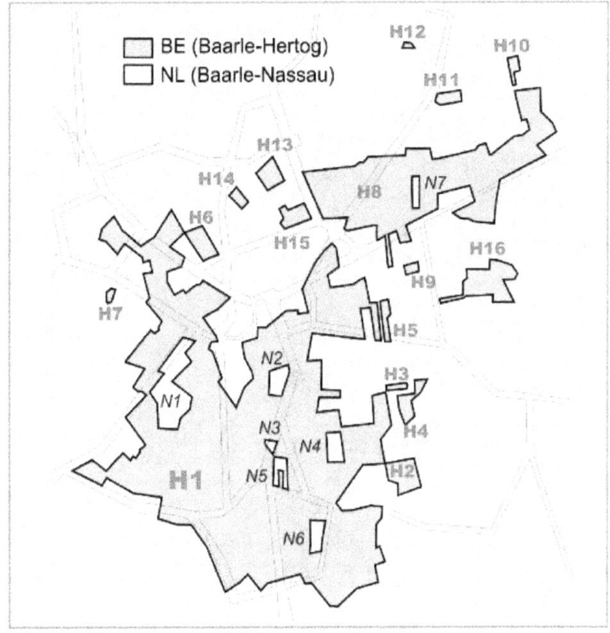

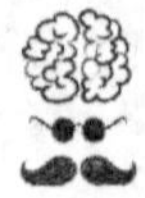

379.

In South Korea, the typical gift for a house-warming party is toilet paper.

380.

Korea invented metal printing type some 200 years before Johannes Gutenberg.

381.

The Korean alphabet, created in 1443, was inspired by the shapes of the vocal organs. Today it consists of 24 letters in South Korea and 40 in North Korea.

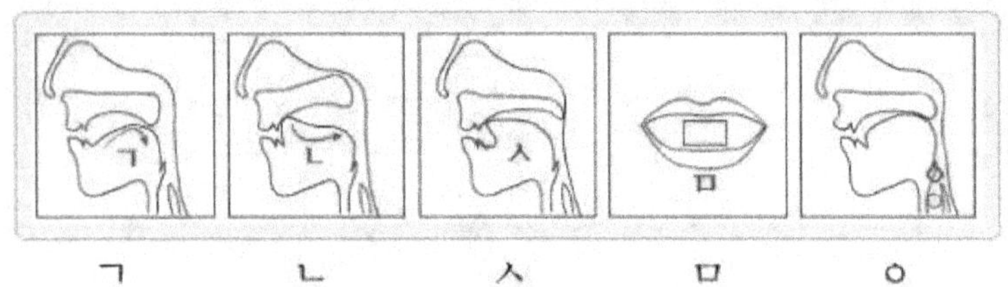

382.

Up until 1882, Korea had no national flag.

383.

In Japan, it is considered rude to eat or talk on the phone while walking.

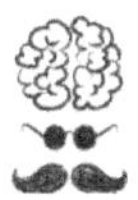

384.

For both religious and practical reasons, the Japanese mostly avoided eating meat for more than twelve centuries. Eating the meat of 4-legged animals was partly or fully prohibited between 675 CE and 1868 CE.

385.

Shitennō-ji is a Buddhist shrine in Osaka, Japan. It is regarded as the first and oldest Buddhist temple in the country.

386.

Sussex and the Isle of Wight were the last places in England to convert to Christianity, in 686 CE.

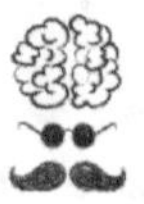

387.

Kabuki theatre is a classical Japanese art of dance-drama, known for the elaborate make-up worn by some of its performers. In 2005, it was proclaimed by UNESCO as an intangible heritage with exceptional universal value. It was founded in 1603 by a troupe of female dancers who played both male and female roles. Women's kabuki was banned in 1629 for being too erotic and ever since this form of theatre has only had male actors.

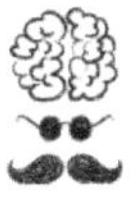

388.

Isle of Sark is one of the Channel Islands, off the coast of Normandy, France. It is unique for being a royal fief with its own set of laws based on Norman law and its own parliament. Sark has a population of about 500 and, including the nearby island of Brecqhou, an area of 5.4 km^2 (2.1 square miles). Sark is one of the few remaining carless places worldwide, where only tractors and horse-drawn carriages are allowed. Up until the constitutional reforms of 2008, the head of the feudal government was called the Seigneur of Sark (in the case of a woman, the title was Dame).

389.

Counterintuitively, Seattle, USA, is further north than Montreal, Canada; the tiny Mediterranean country of Monaco is further north than Boston, USA; and Barcelona, Spain, than Beijing, China.

390.

Valentine's Day in Japan is celebrated quite differently than in the rest of the world: it is women who give gifts to men, habitually in the form of chocolates or cookies. On 14 March, exactly a month after Valentine's Day, is White Day, when men are expected to reciprocate with gifts worth at least three times more than what they received on 14 February.

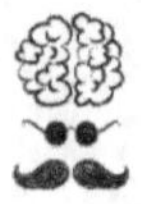

391.

In some Japanese cities, in the vicinity of temples no advertisements can be in red, including Coca-Cola and McDonald's.

392.

The United Kingdom is famous for paying its debts. A few years ago, it repaid bonds from the 1720 South Sea Bubble, the Napoleonic Wars, the Crimean War, and World War I.

393.

More vegetarians live in India (31% of the Indian population) than in the rest of the world.

394.

Maine is the only US state to border just one state.

395.

Norway plans to ban sales of petrol and diesel cars from 2025.

396.

The old walled city of Jerusalem, Israel, has four quarters: Jewish, Christian, Muslim, and Armenian.

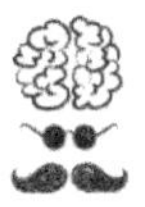

397.

Until 2017, land in Barbuda was owned collectively by all citizens: no money involved, one could claim a piece of land by just putting up a fence.

398.

So far, eight US Presidents were left-handed: James Garfield, Herbert Hoover, Harry Truman, Gerald Ford, Ronald Reagan, George H.W. Bush, Bill Clinton, and Barack Obama.

399.

Which town would you like to visit: Dull (Scotland), Boring (Oregon, USA), or Bland (Australia)? They do not sound very interesting, do they?

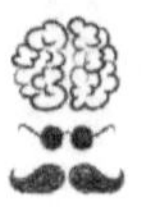

400.

Dunkin' Donuts, Starbucks, and KFC have all tried and failed in Israel. In early 2020, KFC re-entered the country – results remain to be seen.

401.

Saudi Arabia is planning a futuristic megacity, "Neom", which will have its own artificial moon. The $500 billion project was introduced in 2017 by Saudi Arabia's Crown Prince Mohammed bin Salman. It is planned to include 450 km (280 mi) of Red Sea coastline, which would make it a major vacation destination – 8 hours by plane from anywhere in the world, as calculated by the consultants. Neom will span a total area of 26,500 km^2 (over 10,000 sq. mi) across three countries, including territories from north-western Saudi Arabia, Egypt, and Jordan.

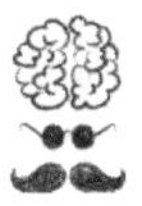

402.

The Sovereign Military Order of Malta, officially the Sovereign Military Hospitaller Order of Saint John of Jerusalem, of Rhodes, and of Malta, is dubbed "the smallest sovereign state in the world".

403.

For Greeks, Cypriots, and others in the Orthodox tradition, St Basil is the saint associated with Santa Claus as opposed to the western tradition of St Nicholas.

404.

The largest swimming pool worldwide is in Egypt. Citystars Sharm El Sheikh measures 96,800 m^2 (1,042,000 sq. ft). It opened in 2015 and is full of seawater.

405.

The Turkish province of Batman is collecting signatures to redraw its borders in the shape of superhero Batman's logo. Over 26,000 people signed since 2018.

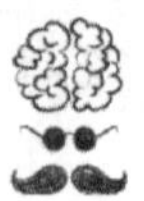

406.

The Western Wall (aka as Wailing Wall, Kosel, or Kotel) in Jerusalem, Israel, is a holy place for Jews. It is a common practice for pilgrims and tourists to put into the cracks of the Wall prayers written on paper. It is also possible to send a prayer to the Western Wall via e-mail, fax, and text messaging; the note is then printed out and placed in the Wall. Every few months, the prayers are collected and buried in the Jewish cemetery on the Mount of Olives.

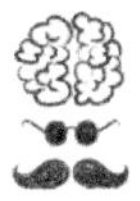

407.

The Colosseum or Coliseum is also known as the Flavian Amphitheatre. At the time it was inaugurated, in 80 CE, the Coliseum was the largest amphitheatre ever built with capacity of 87,000 spectators.

408.

Phone books in Iceland are ordered by first name. The entire culture is based on a first name: patients call their doctor by first name, employees address their bosses by first name, etc.

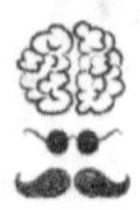

409.

Baron Carl Gustaf Emil Mannerheim (1867-1951) was a Finnish military leader and politician who served as Regent of Finland (1918-1919), commander-in-chief during World War II, Marshal of Finland, and the sixth president of Finland (1944-46). In a 2004 Finnish survey, Mannerheim was voted the greatest Finn of all time. An obscure fact: he learned to speak fluent Finnish only in his fifties.

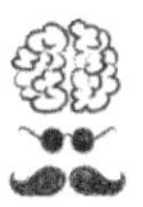

410.

The Incas built Machu Picchu in nowadays southern Peru around 1450 CE. It was deserted a century later at the time of the Spanish conquest. Machu Picchu was kept a secret from the Spanish colonisers and was discovered only in 1911 by US archaeologist Hiram Bingham. The name of the site is usually interpreted as "old mountain" – from Quechua words "machu" (meaning "old") and "picchu" (meaning "pyramid or cone").

411.

Switzerland has its own traditional way of celebrating Easter. There, it is the cuckoo that brings the Easter eggs.

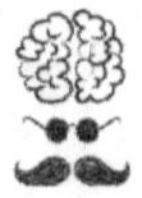

412.

In India, gold has always been a symbol of prosperity. Indian housewives hold over 10 percent of the world gold, more than the reserves of the International Monetary Fund, the United States of America, Germany, and Switzerland combined.

413.

Every first name in Iceland that is not on the government's official list of 3,565 names must be pre-approved by the Icelandic Naming Committee. The goal is to conserve the Icelandic language and to prevent laughable and absurd names.

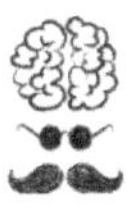

414.

According to Demographia's World Urban Areas report, at the time of writing, there are now 113 urban areas in China that surpass the one-million population threshold. To give you perspective, North America and the European Union combined have 114 urban areas that surpass one million people.

415.

Between 1915 and 1989, beer was illegal in Iceland. The reasons were mainly political as the country was struggling to gain independence from Denmark, and beer was directly associated with the Danish lifestyle. At the time, drinking beer was considered unpatriotic. Beer was finally legalized on 1 March 1989.

416.

Until 1987, when the government in Iceland operated the country's only television station, nothing aired on Thursdays. And because July was considered a vacation month in the country, until 1983, the entire July turned into TV downtime. The ban was in place so residents would get out and socialize. The exact effect of this ban has not been quantified, but perhaps it is part of the reason why Iceland publishes the most books per capita in the world.

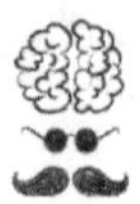

417.

McDonald's opened the doors of its first restaurant in Russia (then USSR) on 31 January 1990. With 900 seats, it was the largest McDonald's in the world at the time. Some 27,000 Russians applied to work at the first McDonald's in Russia, with 630 eventually hired. All this in a country where unemployment did not officially exist.

418.

Worldwide, there are only four national anthems that have no official lyrics: the ones of Spain, San Marino, Bosnia and Herzegovina, and Kosovo.

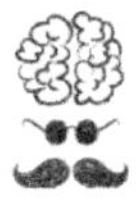

419.

Vietnam is the world's largest black pepper producer and exporter, accounting for nearly half of the global output.

420.

Simón Bolívar (1783-1830), aka El Libertador ("The Liberator" in Spanish), was a Venezuelan political leader who headed the revolutions against Spanish rule in the Viceroyalty of New Granada. For a few years, he was simultaneously president of Gran Colombia (present-day Venezuela, Colombia, Panama, and Ecuador), Peru, and Bolivia.

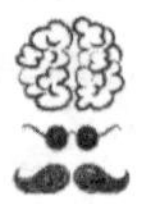

421.

The Nigerian film industry, also known as Nollywood, produces about 50 movies per week, more than Hollywood in the United States. Nollywood is second only to India's Bollywood.

422.

Many world maps leave out New Zealand – so many that there is a website dedicated to this phenomenon: http://worldmapswithout.nz/. Awkwardly, the list of organizations having forgotten to include New Zealand on their world map includes the government of New Zealand...

423.

There are 365 churches in Malta: one for each day of the year!

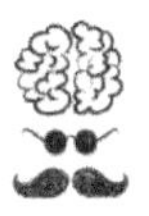

424.

South Africa holds the record with three capitals: Pretoria (administrative and executive capital), Cape Town (legislative capital), and Bloemfontein (judicial capital). Several other countries have two capital cities:

* Benin: Porto-Novo (official capital; seat of legislature) and Cotonou (de facto seat of government; seat of judicial bodies);

* Bolivia: Sucre (official, constitutional capital; seat of national judiciary) and La Paz (seat of national executive, legislative, and electoral bodies);

* Burundi: Gitega (official, constitutional capital) and Bujumbura (seat of national executive);

* Chile: Santiago (official capital; seat of national administrative and judicial bodies) and Valparaíso (seat of national legislature);

* Côte d'Ivoire: Yamoussoukro (official capital) and Abidjan (de facto seat of government);

* Czech Republic: Prague (official capital, seat of national administrative and legislative bodies) and Brno (seat of national judiciary bodies);

* Dominican Republic: Santo Domingo (official capital, seat of all national administrative and legislative bodies and some judiciary bodies) and Santo Domingo Oeste (seat of the Constitutional Court and the Central Electoral Board);

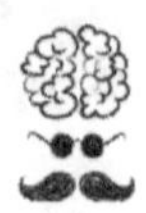

- Eswatini, officially the Kingdom of Eswatini formerly known as Swaziland: Mbabane (administrative capital) and Lobamba (legislative and royal capital);

- Honduras: Tegucigalpa (de facto capital) and Comayagüela (together with Tegucigalpa, the two cities constitute the Municipality of the Central District, which is the official constitutional capital);

- Malaysia: Kuala Lumpur (official and royal capital; seat of national legislature) and Putrajaya (administrative centre and seat of national judiciary);

- Montenegro: Podgorica (official capital) and Cetinje (seat of the President of Montenegro);

- Netherlands: Amsterdam (de jure capital under the Constitution of the Netherlands) and The Hague (seat of government);

- Sri Lanka: Sri Jayawardenepura Kotte (official capital and seat of national legislature) and Colombo (de facto seat of national executive and judicial bodies);

- Tanzania: Dodoma (official and legislative capital) and Dar es Salaam (de facto seat of government; seat of judicial bodies);

- Western Sahara (SADR): Laayoune (declared capital) and Tifariti (temporary capital);

- Yemen: Sana'a (internationally recognized capital, controlled by the Houthis) and Aden (temporary capital).

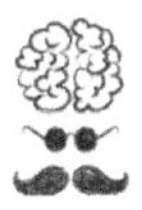

425.

Kazakhstan is the largest landlocked country in the world with an area of 2,724,900 km² (1,052,100 sq. mi). Kazakhstan is located in Central Asia and borders five countries: China, Kyrgyzstan, Russia, Turkmenistan, and Uzbekistan.

426.

44 out of the 50 US states are partitioned entirely into counties. Louisiana comprises 64 equivalent parishes, while Alaska is partitioned into 19 equivalent boroughs and 10 sparsely populated census areas. Virginia, Maryland, Missouri, and Nevada are each composed entirely of counties and independent cities.

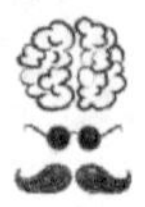

427.

US Founding Fathers drank Madeira wine after the signing of the Declaration of Independence.

428.

In 2019, the Dutch government stopped calling itself Holland and instead started using only its real name – The Netherlands – as part of an attempted update of its global image.

429.

Sanna Mirella Marin (born on 16 November 1985) is a Finnish politician who has been serving as the Prime Minister of Finland since 10 December 2019. At age 34, Marin became both the world's youngest serving state leader at the time (although she lost that position to Austria's Sebastian Kurz a few weeks later) and Finland's youngest-ever prime minister.

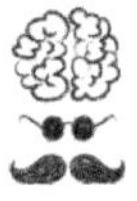

430.

Andorra increased its population 12-fold between 1950 and 2010.

431.

The Vennbahn is an obsolete 19th-century railway line built across what was then German territory. Today, it is entirely in Belgium because the track bed of the line, as well as the stations, were made Belgian territory in 1919 by the Treaty of Versailles. This resulted in creating six German exclaves on the Vennbahn's western side, of which five still remain.

432.

California, Delaware, Florida, Oregon, Idaho, Kansas, Nevada, and New Hampshire are all towns in Ohio, USA.

433.

The equator passes through the territory of thirteen countries: Ecuador, Gabon, Republic of the Congo, Democratic Republic of the Congo, Colombia, Brazil, Sao Tome & Principe, Uganda, Kenya, Somalia, Maldives, Indonesia, and Kiribati.

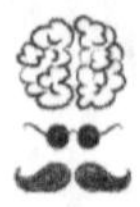

434.

The Baltic Way or Baltic Chain (aka Chain of Freedom) was a peaceful political protest that took place on 23 August 1989. Two million protesters held their hands to form a human chain measuring 676 kilometres (420 mi) across the three Baltic States – Estonia, Latvia, and Lithuania, at the time constituent republics of the Soviet Union. The USSR would eventually be dissolved in 1991.

435.

Pakistan was founded in 1947. No Pakistani government had served its full term until 2013.

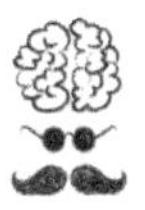

436.

As of this writing, Russia is the largest market for Pepsi outside the USA. Pepsi started exporting its syrup to USSR in 1972 and locked Coca-Cola out of the Soviet market for some 15 years. It was the first company from a capitalist country offering a popular consumer product in the Soviet Union. Soviet roubles were not traded internationally since Moscow forbade currency exports and a barter deal was negotiated: Pepsi concentrate was swapped for Stolichnaya vodka and distribution rights in the USA. It all ended in 1980, when the USA boycotted Soviet products, which included vodka, because of the USSR's invasion of Afghanistan. So, the Soviets traded Pepsi an entire military fleet for lots of soda. Pepsi obtained 17 submarines, a cruiser, a frigate, and a destroyer, along with the exclusive rights to open Pizza Hut restaurants in the USSR. This made Pepsi the 6th most powerful navy in the world, before they on-sold the vessels for scrap recycling. Maybe you are wondering what Pepsi's arch-rival was doing at this time. In 1986, Coca-Cola production finally began in the Soviet Union again through a barter deal: Soviet Lada cars were swapped for the concentrate. It was not a profitable agreement since it took three days to make each car road-worthy before putting it on the European market.

437.

Shamanism is one of the most popular religions in Mongolia.

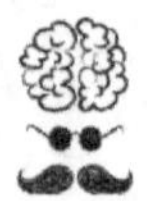

438.

In 2018, hundreds of doctors in Quebec, Canada, protested against their pay raises, saying they already make too much money.

439.

Worldwide, high-school teachers are best paid in Luxembourg.

440.

Australian citizens are legally entitled to a portrait of Queen Elizabeth II. With one simple email, they can acquire a free portrait of Her Majesty the Queen.

441.

In 1980, a third of the world's population lived in countries ruled by Marxist parties.

442.

John Tyler (1790-1862) was the 10th US President. As of this writing, two of his grandchildren are still alive. Their father, Lyon Gardiner Tyler, one of President Tyler's fifteen kids, was born in 1853. He fathered Lyon Gardiner Tyler Jr. in 1924, and Harrison Ruffin Tyler in 1928.

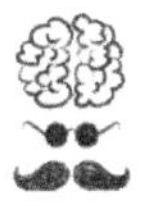

443.

In August 2019, US President Donald Trump confirmed he was considering buying Greenland from Denmark for strategic reasons. Greenland is the world's largest island if we don't consider the continent Australia. US presidents have paid for territories before. In 1803, Thomas Jefferson bought huge tracts of land from France for $15 million in the so-called Louisiana Purchase. In 1867, Andrew Johnson paid Russia $7.2 million for Alaska. A territory has also been purchased from Denmark: in 1917, Woodrow Wilson bought the Danish West Indies for $25 million, renaming them the US Virgin Islands.

444.

The Canadian $2 coin, aka the "toonie", was the world's first glow-in-the-dark coin to enter into circulation in 2017. The coin was created to mark the 150th anniversary of Canada.

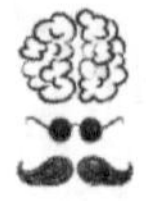

445.

Since 2018, Singapore's Changi Airport has been offering its passengers a slide ride that takes them to the gate.

446.

In 2013, the Vatican withdrew medals commemorating Francis's papacy after misspelling the name of Jesus as "Lesus". The medals – 200 in gold, 3,000 in silver and 3,000 in bronze – were swiftly recalled from the Vatican Publishing House in St Peter's Square.

447.

Throughout Europe, consumer prices were highest in Iceland, followed by Switzerland, Norway, and Denmark, according to 2018 Eurostat data.

448.

In 1952, the Knesset (Israeli parliament) passed the Israeli nationality law and Israel began issuing passports. The first passport was issued to Golda Meir, who at the time worked for the Jewish Agency and was to become Israel's 4th Prime Minister.

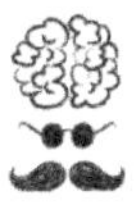

449.

There are many sovereign countries named after people. I am sure you do not know them all:

* Bolivia – Simón Bolívar;

* China – Emperor Qin (pronounced "Chin") of the Qin Dynasty;

* Colombia – Christopher Columbus;

* Dominican Republic – Saint Dominic;

* El Salvador – Jesus (literally from Spanish, The Saviour);

* Eswatini (former Swaziland) – King Mswati II;

* Israel – Jacob, aka Israel;

* Jordan (The Hashemite Kingdom of) – Hashim ibn Abd Manaf (for "Hashemite"); the name Jordan comes from the Jordan River;

* Kiribati – Thomas Gilbert ("Kiribati" is the rendition of "Gilberts" in Gilbertese – an Austronesian language spoken mainly in Kiribati);

* Liechtenstein – Princely Family of Liechtenstein;

* Marshall Islands – John Marshall;

* Mauritius – Maurice of Nassau, Prince of Orange;

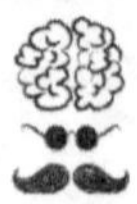

- Mozambique – Mussa Bin Bique;

- Nicaragua – The Nicarao, a Mesoamerican people that migrated south from Mexico;

- Peru – Birú, a local ruler from the 16th century;

- Philippines – King Philip II of Spain;

- Saint Kitts and Nevis - Saint Christopher;

- Saint Lucia – Saint Lucy;

- Saint Vincent and the Grenadines – Saint Vincent of Saragossa;

- San Marino – Saint Marinus;

- São Tomé and Príncipe - Saint Thomas and Prince of Portugal;

- Saudi Arabia – Muhammad bin Saud;

- Seychelles – Jean Moreau de Séchelles;

- Solomon Islands – King Solomon of Israel and Judah;

- United States of America – Amerigo Vespucci;

- Uzbekistan – Öz Beg Khan;

- Venezuela (The Bolivarian Republic of) – Simón Bolívar (for "Bolivarian") and the name Venezuela is derived from Venice.

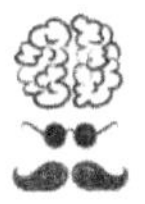

450.

The Hong Kong-Zhuhai-Macau Bridge is a 55-kilometre (34 mi) bridge/tunnel complex comprising three cable-stayed bridges, four artificial islands, and an undersea tunnel. As of this writing, it is the longest cross-sea bridge on the planet.

451.

Cannabis in California, USA, has been legal for recreational use since late 2016. In mid-2019, however, San Francisco, California, became the first major city to ban vaping.

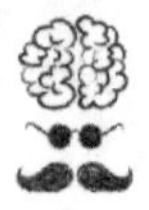

452.

The Bajau, a people of the Malay Archipelago, spend almost all of their lives at sea. They live either on boats or in huts perched on stilts on shallow reefs and migrate from place to place in flotillas that carry entire clans. They survive on a diet composed almost entirely of seafood, which they gather by spending 60% of their working day underwater. They sometimes descend more than 70 m (230 ft) and can stay submerged for up to five minutes. Since the Bajau have lived like this for a long time (historical evidence suggests at least 1,000 years), many researchers have speculated that they carry genetic traits that adapt them to their remarkable lifestyle. A 2018 report of the University of California, USA, confirmed their genes have several mutations favouring the diving lifestyle and their spleens are 50% larger than those of members of neighbouring tribes. The spleen is an organ that acts as an emergency reserve of oxygenated red blood cells and when it contracts, an increased supply of these cells is released into the bloodstream.

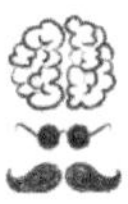

453.

In China, Singapore, and Taiwan, there is a baby boom every 12 years because a superstition "guarantees" that children born in the Year of the Dragon will be more successful in life. As a matter of fact, "dragon" children in China enjoy higher admission test scores and are more likely to go to university than similar-age kids born in other Chinese zodiac years. Researchers from Louisiana State University (USA) examined the phenomenon and claim that the parents of dragon children have sky-high expectations of their children and invest in them more intensely. In the end, the higher expectations produce this self-fulfilling prophecy.

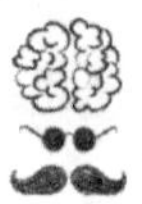

454.

In the 19th century, Australia proclaimed as its highest spot the wrong place, Mount Kosciuszko. Subsequent measurements proved it to be a bit lower than its neighbour, Mount Townsend. In 1892, the New South Wales Lands Department resolved the embarrassing situation by simply swapping the names of the peaks. Ever since, Mount Kosciuszko has remained the name of the highest peak of Australia, and Mount Townsend holds the second place.

455.

As of today, Quebec, Canada, is the only fortified city in North America north of Mexico that still has walls.

456.

As of this writing, Austria, Belgium, and Sweden have effectively stopped using coal power plants.

457.

In 2018, Scotland introduced a minimum price of 50 pence ($0.60 or €0.55) per unit of alcohol.

458.

In 2012, Switzerland held a referendum on the federal initiative "six weeks of vacation for everyone". Two-thirds of the voters said "no".

459.

Spain holds the record of being mentioned in 13 national anthems of other countries. France is second, with 8 mentions.

460.

In 2020, Maldives became the first country to introduce a frequent visitors' program.

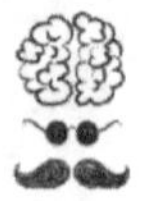

461.

In the 2018 presidential elections in Egypt, more than one million Egyptians struck out the names of both contenders and cast their ballot for Mohamed Salah (writing his name on the ballot). Salah is a widely popular Egyptian footballer who played a decisive role in qualifying Egypt for the 2018 World Cup. He did not participate in the elections yet got second place.

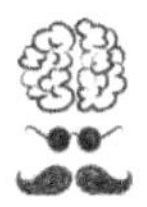

462.

According to INRIX 2019 Global Traffic Scorecard, the cities where drivers spent most hours in traffic jams in 2018 were Bogota, Colombia, and Rio de Janeiro, Brazil: 191 and 190 hours per year, respectively.

463.

In Finland, when one receives a PhD diploma, they are also given a top hat and a sword for the ceremony.

###

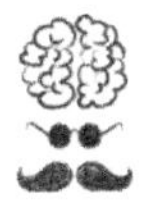

VERIFICATION PROCESS

To start with, however a great read Wikipedia is, I have never used it to confirm facts; I instead checked the sources listed there and evaluated them.

Anything science-related like "Ruby is red and sapphire is blue. Yet, both gemstones are varieties of the same mineral – corundum." would need to be confirmed by at least two (preferably three) separate scientific publications, be it on paper or online of the sort of

http://www.science.gov/,
http://www.nasa.gov/,
http://www.britannica.com/,
http://www.sciencemag.org/,
https://www.newscientist.com/,
https://www.genome.gov/education/,
http://www.howstuffworks.com/,
http://www.merriam-webster.com/.

The scientific publications and websites of the best universities worldwide are also consistently checked (excerpt from the list): University of Cambridge, Stanford University, University of Oxford, California Institute of

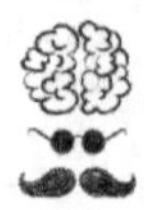

Technology, Massachusetts Institute of Technology, Harvard University, Princeton University, Imperial College London, ETH Zurich – Swiss Federal Institute of Technology, Yale University, Columbia University, University of Toronto, Humboldt University of Berlin, University of Tokyo, Heidelberg University, University of Melbourne, Peking University etc.

For events or facts of the type "The speed record for steam locomotives is 200.4 km/h (124.5 mph). It remains unbroken since 1938.", I checked at least three reputable newspaper articles and confirmed television reports. Example for newspapers/TV channels used to verify events: The New York Times, Washington Post, Wall Street Journal, The Guardian, The Economist, Financial Times, Times of India, Le Monde, The Sydney Morning Herald, Frankfurter Allgemeine Zeitung, Bloomberg, Al Jazeera, Reuters, Associated Press, BBC, TV5 MONDE, CNN, etc.

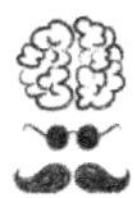

ACKNOWLEDGEMENTS

This book is dedicated to my family: my loving wife, Anna, my curious and restless sons, Pavel and Nikolay, and my mother, Maria, who sparked my interest in reading. Thank you for being so patient with me during the lengthy process of writing. You are my inspiration!

Many thanks to my editor, Andrea Leitenberger, to all test readers, friends, and colleagues who provided vital feedback and constructive criticism.

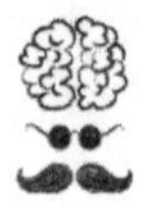

ZEALOUS TEST READERS:

Alexandra Oliveira-Jones

Brian Power

Cathy Ciszek

Dimitar Dimitrov

Elaine Fitt

Elijah Zhai

Eva Goulas

Gayle Hoefker

Heather Wilkinson

Istvan Kovacs

Jackie Milne

Jess Bauldry

Kalina Simeonova

Linda Van Ras

Liz Read

Marina Heda

Matthew E. McGoey

Robert Pernetta

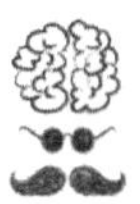

ABOUT THE AUTHOR

Born in Bulgaria, I have lived in places like Germany, Belgium, and Iraq, before settling down with my family in Luxembourg. With varied interests, I have always suffered from an insatiable appetite for facts stemming from an unrestrainable intellectual curiosity. It has undoubtedly influenced my academic background and career: after acquiring Master degrees in Greek Philology, German and English Translation, I graduated in Crisis Management and Diplomacy, and most recently undertook an MBA. Member of MENSA.

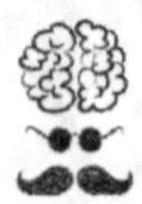

My career has been equally broad and diverse, swinging from that of an army paratrooper and a military intelligence analyst; through to that of a civil servant with the European Commission, and presently, that of a clerk, performing purely financial tasks in a major bank.

My hobbies include scuba diving, travelling, and learning foreign languages.

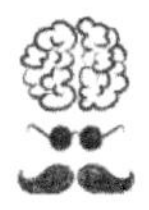

MY BOOKS ON AMAZON

1123 Hard To Believe Facts

Which Is NOT True? - The Quiz Book

Fascinating Facts for the Whole Family
(also in audio format)

853 Hard To Believe Facts

523 Hard To Believe Facts (also in audio format)

323 Disturbing Facts about Our World

CONNECT WITH NAYDEN KOSTOV

Email: n.kostov@raiseyourbrain.com

Facebook: https://www.facebook.com/raiseyourbrain/

Twitter: @RaiseYourBrain

Instagram: RaiseYourBrain

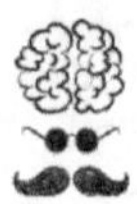

I hope you have enjoyed this book. I would greatly appreciate it if you would write your honest review on Amazon and GoodReads.

You could also check out my other books and download a free sample from my website www.RaiseYourBrain.com:

1123 Hard To Believe Facts

Which Is NOT True? - The Quiz Book

Fascinating Facts for the Whole Family

853 Hard To Believe Facts

523 Hard To Believe Facts

323 Disturbing Facts about Our World

There you could also subscribe to my newsletter and learn first about my future projects.